D0642647

Edward James Lennox

Edward James Lennox as represented in C. Blackett Robinson's
History of Toronto and County of York Ontario (1885).

Metropolitan Toronto Reference Library

Edward James Lennox
"Builder of Toronto"

Marilyn M. Litvak

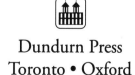

Dundurn Press
Toronto • Oxford

Copyright © Marilyn Litvak, 1995

All rights reserved. No part of this publication may be reproduced, stored in a retrieval system, or transmitted in any form or by any means, electronic, mechanical, photocopying, recording, or otherwise (except brief passages for purposes of review), without the prior permission of Dundurn Press Limited. Permission to photocopy should be requested from the Canadian Reprography Collective.

Edited by Doris Cowan
Printed and bound in Canada by Webcom

The publisher wishes to acknowledge the generous assistance and ongoing support of the **Canada Council**, the **Book Publishing Industry Development Program** of the **Department of Canadian Heritage**, the **Ontario Arts Council**, the **Ontario Publishing Centre** of the **Ministry of Citizenship, Culture and Recreation**, and the **Ontario Heritage Foundation.**
    Care has been taken to trace the ownership of copyright material used in the text (including the illustrations). The author and publisher welcome any information enabling them to rectify any reference or credit in subsequent editions.

J. Kirk Howard, Publisher

Canadian Cataloguing in Publication Data
Litvak, Marilyn
    Edward James Lennox : "builder of Toronto"

Includes bibliographical references and index.
ISBN 1-55002-204-0

1. Lennox, Edward James, 1854–1933. 2. Architecture, Modern –
19th century – Ontario – Toronto. 3. Architecture, Modern – 20th
century – Ontario – Toronto. 4. Toronto (Ont.) – Buildings, structures,
etc. 5. Architects – Ontario – Toronto – Biography. I. Title.

NA749.L44L57 1995   720'.92   C93-094433-X

Dundurn Press Limited	Dundurn Distribution	Dundurn Press Limited
2181 Queen Street East	73 Lime Walk	1823 Maryland Avenue
Suite 301	Headington, Oxford	P.O. Box 1000
Toronto, Canada	England	Niagara Falls, N.Y.
M4E 1E5	OX3 7AD	U.S.A. 14302-1000

for

Isaiah & Matthew

Contents

PREFACE

dward James Lennox's architecture is still a part of Toronto's daily life, yet few people recognize the name of the man who was once called "the builder of Toronto." Lennox was responsible for such key monuments as Old City Hall, the Bank of Toronto on Yonge Street, Casa Loma, and St. Paul's Anglican Church on Bloor Street East. During the four decades between 1876 and 1917 his output was prodigious. Some of his work has been highlighted in general texts, and articles have been written over the years in praise of Lennox and his architecture, but this is the first time, in the more than sixty years since his death, that a book has been devoted exclusively to his work.

My chief concern has been to convey a sense of Lennox's importance in Toronto's architectural history, and to show how his buildings represent his interpretation of contemporary architectural trends.

The task of assembling the photographs, drawings, perspectives, and other records of Lennox's work was an enormous one. Many buildings known to have been built by Lennox had not been documented. In addition, some information about Lennox and his buildings contained in books, articles, and repositories (building inventories, for instance) proved to be incorrect. For example, various birth dates are given for Lennox: 1854, 1855, and 1856 all appear in different books and articles. However, on the evidence of the chronology of his architectural training, it appears that Lennox's gravestone in St. James' Cemetery on Parliament Street gives the correct year – 1854.

The documents are also at variance in their accounts of Lennox's early practice. For decades his partner was identified as McGaw, sometimes McCaw, with no first name or initials, and their partnership was noted as having dissolved in 1882. It was not until the 1980s that the full and correct name was established: Lennox's architectural partner was William Frederick McCaw[1] and it is clear from the author's findings that Lennox set out on his own in 1881. Additionally, buildings have been attributed to Lennox which simply are not his – Massey Hall is a good example. It was not designed by Lennox; indeed, it was not even supervised by him. However, once in print, an error in fact becomes a "fact" in error and develops a life of its own. In many ways this project was motivated by the desire to set the record straight, although I am sure I too have been guilty of accepting information that will eventually be proved incorrect.

A search of textual materials, photographs, and drawings related to Lennox and his work was undertaken at such institutions as the Metropolitan Toronto Reference Library, Toronto Historical Board, Toronto City Hall Archives, Ontario Hydro Archives, Federal Department of the Environment (Canadian Historic Buildings Inventory), National Archives of Canada, Ontario Ministry of Culture, Tourism and Recreation, the Niagara Parks Commission, and the Archives of Ontario. I also interviewed a number of Lennox's descendants.

One of Toronto's enthusiastic architectural conservationists, Kent Rawson, generously gave me access to his research concerning late nineteenth-century advertisements in Toronto newspapers, specifically, lists of architectural calls for tender. This was most helpful in verifying Lennox's responsibility for particular buildings and in assigning dates to them, especially when dealing with the early part of Lennox's career.

Early Toronto city records were searched, and on-site investigation of extant buildings was undertaken. The buildings (including the interior of Lennox's own home) were photographed. Photographs of destroyed buildings have been reproduced from material such as books, periodicals, slides, and negatives held by various public and private institutions. More than one hundred photographs of Lennox's buildings were amassed.

Most of the buildings I could verify as Lennox's works are included in the text and are discussed chronologically; his additions and/or renovations to buildings, unless of major importance to Toronto or indicative of a change in stylistic orientation, are not discussed. Dates assigned to buildings were based on Lennox's architectural drawings, building permits, calls for tender, listings in city directories, letters, transcripts, and architectural specifications. If no such evidence was available, dates assigned by other writers were accepted and they have been so credited. In 1905 Lennox himself published a promotional portfolio in which many of his buildings are illustrated. As a record of his work it is both helpful and problematic in that the illustrations bear only incomplete addresses and no dates. Lennox left no treatises on architectural theories, no papers outlining his career, no personal papers. He devoted his time to his career, and the writing he did was specific to business dealings, with the exception of a short article published for the purpose of raising funds for the Toronto General Hospital (see Appendix A). When he first started practising architecture in 1876, Toronto's population was a little more than 70,000. By the time he had completed the building of his home, Lenwil, in 1915, Toronto, with a population approaching half a million, had become a significant metropolis. During those forty years building technologies, systems of transportation, and the means of generating power changed, but the changes had very little effect on Lennox's architectural vision.

To the end of his life, Lennox was a resolute individualist. While he was not a pioneer of modern design, his traditionalist structures were nonetheless highly original. He designed with an artist's eye and a sense of theatre; his talent as an architect rested in the power of his imagination and the strength of his artistic will – qualities that ultimately allowed him to put his unique stamp on all his work and set his buildings apart from others.

ACKNOWLEDGMENTS

This project, though difficult, was above all gratifying. A research grant was provided by the Ontario Heritage Foundation and I had the help and encouragement of some of the most considerate people. My thanks go to Jane Aitken, Paul Dilse, Mr. and Mrs. P. Eckardt, William Gilpin, Alec Keefer, Sharon Kish, John Yudelman; Karen Teeple, Steve Mackinnon, and other members of the City of Toronto Archives; Karen Bergsteinsson, Bill Cooper, Katrin Cooper, and Christine Niarchos-Bourolias of the Ontario Archives; Amy Lu, William Parker, Alan Walker, Tanya Henley, and other members of the staff of Metropolitan Toronto Reference Library; the Toronto Historical Board; Casa Loma; the Niagara Parks Commission; Ed Dover and Rosa Paparella of the Ontario Hydro Archives; Alex D. Camp of St. Paul's Anglican Church Archives; Sister Victoria of Sisters Servants of Mary Immaculate Christ the King; and John O'Brien, who did a superb job photographing some of Lennox's extant work.

My very special thanks go to my husband Isaiah Alan Litvak. This book would never have been completed without his help, love, patience, and encouragement.

INTRODUCTION

he Toronto into which Lennox was born in the year 1854 was a city of wharfs, churches, schools, and small businesses. The population, according to the provincial census of 1851–52, was just over thirty thousand. More than a third of Toronto's population at that time were Irish born. Both of Lennox's parents were born in the County of Antrim, near Belfast, but they did not meet until they arrived in Toronto. Lennox's father had come to Upper Canada in 1832; he settled in Toronto, started a general produce business, speculated in real estate, and for about twenty years owned and ran a hotel on Francis Street (Francis Street ran north from King, opposite St. Lawrence Hall).

As a young child, Lennox was not known for his scholarly ability. But he exhibited strong artistic talent and was determined to become an architect.[1] However, his father did not approve and it was only after much pleading that he was permitted to attend architectural drawing class at the Mechanics' Institute.[2] It was there his talent was recognized. "Though he was one of the youngest among experienced and older students, he carried off first prize and diploma at the head of about sixty pupils."[3]

He was seventeen years of age at the time and, indeed, much younger than any of his fellow students, most of whom were experienced mechanics. Once having proved his ability and his determination, he was allowed to study architecture. His father helped him secure a place in the office of Toronto architect William Irving (1830–83), where he remained for five years.[4]

Irving's architectural style had considerable impact on the young Lennox. Born in Edinburgh, Scotland, Irving was the son of a contractor and stone carver;[5] he had arrived in Toronto in the early 1850s and joined the shop of Joseph Sheard (1813–83). Sheard and Irving were responsible for the building of the Ontario Bank, 1862 (Illus. 1 and 2).[6] Reminiscent of an Italian Renaissance palace, the heavily carved surfaces and sculptural elements contributed to its presence and symbolism.

Having completed his apprenticeship, Lennox entered into partnership with William Frederick McCaw in 1876 – an association that lasted until 1881. That year Lennox, or E.J. as he was known to his friends, set out on his own and had the good fortune to marry a well-organized and efficient woman – Emeline, the second daughter of John Wilson of Cobourg, Ontario.[7]

The Lennoxes had four children: Eola Gertrude, Edgar Edward, Mabel Emeline, and Edith May. For thirty years, while the children were growing up, the family lived on Sherbourne Street, a boulevard occupied by Torontonians of wealth and influence. It was not until Lennox was in his mid-fifties that he began to design a grand house for himself and Emeline. The property, two and a half acres just west of Casa Loma, was purchased in 1905, and construction was begun in 1913. He and Emeline called their house "Lenwil" for both of their families – "Len" for Lennox and "wil" for Wilson. The Lennoxes moved into Lenwil in 1915. It was to be one of the last buildings E.J. worked on.

In 1977 Edith May "Maisie" Eckardt, Lennox's youngest daughter, spoke with Colin Vaughan for an article about Lenwil and her father;[8] she was eighty-five at the time. She talked about how exciting it was to move from Sherbourne Street to Lenwil: "There was no other house in Canada like it." When the Lennoxes moved to their grand house on the brow of Wells Hill, Maisie was the only one of the children still home, but by 1916 she was married and gone. Edith May remembered her father and mother's delight in their home and how, as her father grew older, he would walk about the grounds of Lenwil with a parrot on his shoulder.[9]

The picture his daughter Edith May painted of him is rather romantic: a remote figure walking lonely on the brow of Wells Hill – the artist contemplating his life. Lennox was not the contemplative sort. He was action oriented and demanding, and he expected his children to do his bidding. Edgar Edward, interviewed in 1966, recalled that his father "was not what you might call a heart-to-heart man, but he was a good man who believed in the virtues of honesty and integrity, and practised them."[10] His grandchildren do not remember him very well. They have sharper memories of their grandmother. Peter Eckardt, Edith May's son, has fond recollections of outings in his grandparents' chauffeured car, a "1928 Pierce Arrow, 7 passenger Sedan," and remembers his grandmother as a strong woman who made certain that his grandfather was left alone so that he could tend to matters of architecture and business.[11]

Lennox pursued his career vigorously and as early as 1885 he had one of the largest architectural practices of its kind in Canada. What Lennox lacked in eduction, he more than made up for in shrewdness and salesmanship. An able promoter, E.J. was receptive to the press and was most accommodating when it came to having his photo taken (Illus. 4). He was also politically astute. His active membership in such notable organizations as the Masons, the Board of Trade, and Cameron Loyal Orange Lodge was to prove mutually beneficial.[12]

His professional success was such that in 1901 he was able to purchase a building on Bay Street to house his firm (Illus. 133). Lennox's career continued to flourish until 1915, when for some as yet undiscovered reason, he turned away from his practice. By 1917, the firm of E.J. Lennox, Architect was officially closed.[13] Though no longer practising, Lennox continued to consider himself an architect first and foremost. And when legislation was passed in 1931 to provide architects with certification, Lennox applied for and became an accredited architect. The date was 29 September of that same year. At the time, Lennox was seventy-seven years old; his application lists no date of birth and his handwriting was not steady.

E.J. Lennox died on 15 April 1933. His passing was noted in many newspapers (Illus. 3), including the *New York Times,* as well as important architectural journals. His contributions to the City of Toronto, and to his profession, were praised and remembered. In his obituary in the *Telegram,* M. Forsey Page, president of the Ontario Architectural Association, commended Lennox not only for his buildings and his knowledge of modern architectural technologies but also for his willingness to share this knowledge with younger architects.[14] His funeral took place in one of his last great works, St. Paul's Anglican Church on Bloor Street East. E.J.'s good friend of more than forty years, Canon Henry John Cody, rector of St. Paul's, officiated.

E.J. Lennox was an impressive talent who was arrogant, combative, and fearless when it came to speaking his mind. Despite his eccentricities, he was commissioned to design many of Toronto's more notable structures and ultimately became known as the "builder of Toronto." Lennox believed that he was destined to be a great architect. The quantity and quality of his work speak to that conviction.

Illus. 1: Ontario Bank, northeast corner of Wellington and Scott streets, 1862, William Irving and Joseph Sheard (demolished).

Metropolitan Toronto Reference Library

Illus. 2: Ontario Bank. Detail.

Metropolitan Toronto Reference Library

'BUILDER OF TORONTO' E. J. LENNOX PASSES

Famed Architect Had Designed Most of Major City Structures

Edward James Lennox, architect, designer and builder of the city hall, died yesterday. In poor health for several months, he was in his 78th year.

He is said to have done more than any other individual in the building up of Toronto. Among the structures he designed are the city hall, Casa Loma, St. Paul's Anglican church, Bloor St., Massey Hall, the King Edward Hotel, Manning Arcade, old Bond St. church, Erskine United church and others. He also designed and supervised the building of the Electrical Development Co. and Toronto Power Co. plants at Niagara Falls, Ont.

The late Mr. Lennox was born in Toronto of Irish parentage, attended the old Model school, and studied architecture under the late William Irving. He commenced the practice of his profession in Toronto with M. McCaw, but after five years dissolved the partnership, and since had practised alone. He was in his younger days a prominent player on the Tecumsehs' lacrosse team, and the Toronto Lacrosse club.

He was the first man to introduce the eight-hour day in the building trade. It arose out of the troubles of the contractors when erecting the city hall, when he was obliged to take over the work, owing to labor difficulties. The gigantic task was followed by lengthy litigation and afterwards arbitration, as to the fee he was to receive.

A member of St. Paul's Anglican church, of Doric Lodge, A.F. and A.M., Cameron L.O.L., with service to his credit on the board of trade and the Toronto Transportation Commission, the late Mr. Lennox was known and esteemed throughout the city.

He is survived by his widow, Emeline Wilson, one son, Edgar E. Lennox, three daughters, Mrs. D. W. Smart, Mrs. Mabel Ryerson and Mrs. Douglas Eckardt, and seven grandchildren, all of Toronto, as well as a sister, Miss Luella Lennox, and a brother, Charles D. Lennox, both of Toronto.

PROMINENT ARCHITECT DIES
E. J. Lennox, who has designed many of Toronto's outstanding buildings, including the city hall and Casa Loma, died Saturday evening at his home on Walmer Rd. He was at one time transportation commissioner for the city.

Illus. 3: Lennox's obituary in the *Toronto Star*, 17 April 1933.

Metropolitan Toronto Reference Library

Illus. 4: E.J. in 1892 in front of one of his more important works, the Freehold Loan Building, Adelaide Street East, 1889.
Metropolitan Toronto Reference Library

1 Early Practice

OCCIDENT HALL

The first known record of E.J. Lennox as a practising architect is an advertisement in the *Globe,* 15 May 1876 (Illus. 5). At that time he was in partnership with a William Frederick McCaw, and their firm asked for contractors to bid on the erection of Occident Hall, at the southeast corner of Queen and Bathurst streets.[1] McCaw & Lennox developed a successful practice, though they faced stiff competition from a growing number of architectural firms practising in Toronto.[2] The number of advertisements for contracting bids in the *Globe* and *Toronto Telegram* between 1876 and 1881 confirms that McCaw & Lennox were popular and sought after.[3] Their commissions ranged from large churches to school houses in Stratford and Owen Sound; from "commodious" brick villas to commercial properties; from a "first class" hotel on the Island, Toronto Bay, to a summer cottage and the design and construction of 2,000 lineal feet of esplanade and terracing at the lakefront in Parkdale. Only a few of the buildings McCaw & Lennox contracted for have been documented. Occident Hall was a major commission and no mean building in its time. C.P. Mulvany, in his *Toronto, Past and Present until 1882* (published 1884), praised the building as handsome and "unique in its design and furniture."[4] Completed in 1878 (Illus. 6), Occident Hall was a tentative exercise in Second Empire style. The original roof is gone and the building, now called the Big Bop, no longer witnesses the secret meetings of Masons; it now vibrates to the sound of hard rock music.

While building Occident Hall, McCaw & Lennox entered a competition for the laying out and beautifying of "the City Parks, viz, the Queen's Park, High Park, and the Eastern Park," which offered $300 to the winners.[5] Their proposal to the Public Walks and Gardens Committee, dated 17 May 1876, was highly detailed, including a grand promenade, ornamental lamps, a large oval-shaped pond, rockeries, and a great deal more. By 19 June 1876 the committee had chosen the winning plans: "For the Queen's Park: – 1st Prize Plan, bearing the motto 'Manu Forti,' by Messrs. McCaw & Lennox, Toronto."[6] Despite the judges' glowing tributes to their design, the city did not go ahead with the Queen's Park beautification program, and months later McCaw and Lennox had to chase City Hall for their $300 prize.[7]

BOND STREET CONGREGATIONAL CHURCH

The original Bond Street Congregational Church burned to the ground in 1878, and McCaw & Lennox were called on to design a new building.[8] They designed a large, "modern" Gothic building that was 24 metres (80 feet) wide and 27 metres (90 feet) deep and could accommodate some fourteen hundred worshippers (Illus. 7). Its main tower on the southwest corner was about 40 metres (130 feet) high (about thirteen storeys), while the tower to the north side was 20 metres (65 feet) high, exactly half the height of the main tower. The roof of the church was octagonal in shape, and was topped by a similarly shaped ornate monitor (Illus. 8) to allow for ventilation.

Entrance to the church was gained through the towers. The pulpit and choir were on the east side of the auditorium. A gallery, supported on columns which extended up the groined dome, ran round the remaining three sides of the church. The design culminated in a second dome of ornamental stained glass. Emphasis was placed on light and comfort, and (to judge by a photograph of the interior) sight-lines were of equal importance (Illus. 9).

The Bond Street church McCaw & Lennox built no longer exists. It suffered a fate similar to that of its predecessor: late in the evening of 19 September 1981 a fire erupted, and the church, which had for a number of decades been the Evangel Temple, was so badly damaged that it had to be demolished. The land on which it stood was for many years a parking lot.

ERSKINE PRESBYTERIAN CHURCH

McCaw & Lennox's second important 1878 commission was Erskine Presbyterian Church on Elm Street (Illus. 10).[9] Similar in size and shape to the Bond Street church, Erskine Presbyterian was articulated in brick as opposed to stone. The design was infinitely more elegant. To emphasize the importance of the building, its gables were finished with stone caps. The main structure was divided into a vestibule that extended the whole width of the front and an auditorium of about 18 metres (60 feet) in depth. No drawings or photographs of the interior are known to exist; all that remains is a description. The auditorium was designed along the lines of an amphitheatre, with the floor sloping towards a platform and pulpit at the north end. The organ was behind the pulpit, and a gallery supported on iron columns filled in the other three sides. The ceiling above the nave was decorated with moulded ribs and bosses. When the building was partially destroyed by fire in early 1884, it was restored "according to the original plans of the architect, Mr. E.J. Lennox."[10] If McCaw objected to Lennox's taking sole credit for the design, the author found no historical record of his complaint.

HOTEL HANLAN

Late in 1879, McCaw & Lennox were commissioned by the world-famous oarsman Edward "Ned" Hanlan to build a hotel on Toronto Island.[11] Hanlan wanted to create a luxurious resort hotel not unlike those being built in the United States. The firm's advertisement read as follows:

TO CONTRACTORS

> Tenders to be received for the building of a first-class hotel on the Island, Toronto Bay for
> **EDWARD HANLAN, ESQ.**
> Plans and specifications, &c. can be seen at our offices. Builders will be required to give substantiated references and security if required. The lowest or any tender not necessarily accepted. Plans, &c., can be seen on and after the 22nd inst.
> **McCaw & Lennox,**
> Architects, 9 & 10 Imperial Building, Toronto.

A sketch of the Hotel Hanlan (Illus. 11) made soon after it was built shows an elegant structure, symmetrical in plan and articulated in American "stick style."[12] Narrow columns (stickwork-like) held up an almost fragile-looking two-tiered veranda which spanned and encircled the building. False timbers decorated the dormers, and towers, punctuating the three bays, were covered by gently concave sloped roofs. All in all, a handsome structure with its roots firmly planted in nineteenth-century America. A photograph taken some years later indicates that the

Hotel Hanlan, once the preserve of the wealthy, was attempting to appeal to a broader market: note roof advertising (Illus. 12).

Throughout 1880–81 the firm continued to be busy. Their commissions ranged from unpretentious residences[13] to grand villas[14] and a summer "cottage" in Parkdale;[15] from a large brick commercial building "to be erected on Queen-street West"[16] to a much smaller one at the southwest corner of Breadalbane and Yonge Street.[17] The Yonge Street building still exists; its Second Empire–style roof is much more dynamic than the one McCaw & Lennox designed for Occident Hall four years earlier.

During the spring of 1881 Ned Hanlan decided to improve his resort, and called on McCaw & Lennox to build a "Bowling Alley, Billiard Room, and Hall" on Toronto Island. The call for tender for that commission is the last known documentation of the McCaw & Lennox partnership. At some point between June and November of 1881, the partnership dissolved. By November of 1881, Lennox advertised alone in the "Tenders Wanted" column of the *Globe* for contractors to submit bids to erect a "Brick Villa Residence on the Allan property, Shuter-street" (Illus. 13).[18] The advertisement lists E.J.'s address as Nos. 8 & 9, the Manning Block, at the southeast corner of King and Yonge streets. Lennox had moved out of the offices in the Imperial Building on Adelaide Street East; the partnership was at an end, and McCaw's name disappeared from the Toronto directory.

Lennox did not have to wait long for important assignments. The architectural profession was in a state of rapid expansion, and the number of firms kept right on growing, as did the population of Toronto and its inventory of buildings.

A LARGE BRICK WOOLLEN FACTORY AND THE BLOOR STREET BAPTIST CHURCH

By February of 1882 Lennox had been commissioned to erect "a large brick woollen factory" on Front Street East.[19] It may well be the Standard Woollen Mills building, 223–237 Front Street East, which is now part of the Joey and Toby Tanenbaum Opera Centre.[20] And by October he was advertising for bids on the building of a church.[21]

The Bloor Street Baptist Church, 1882 (Illus. 14), an unassuming structure of red brick with stone trim, was located at the southeast corner of Bloor and North (now Bay) streets. It was altogether an exercise in restraint. Its most commanding feature was a handsome square tower with a relatively short four-sided spire and "on one side of it, a circular turret with mock winding-staircase-windows and short spiral roof."[22] The tower was "counterbalanced" by large buttresses and a wing. Leading to the tower and providing access to the church was an entrance covered by open-timbered roof, projecting gables, and wrought-iron gates.

From an 1885 description of the interior, its auditorium appears to have been comparable to that of the Bond Street Congregational Church. "Opposite the entrances is the platform, with the baptistry – entirely constructed of marble – behind, and above, a handsome choir and organ gallery, supported by carved columns. A gallery for the general accommodation of worshippers runs round the other three sides of the building. The ceiling is plastered, with groined ribs, dome-shaped in the centre and ornamented with carved capitals, bosses, etc."[23]

THE BILTON AND CLARKE RESIDENCES

By the end of 1882 Lennox was designing semi-detached residences for Mrs. Bilton on Gerrard Street, 1882–83 (Illus. 15).[24] These are excellent examples of Canadian Queen Anne Revival style. They comprise intricate brickwork, elaborate half-timbering, and two large gables. The semi-detached houses were followed by a residence for an H.E. Clarke at 603 Jarvis Street,[25] 1882–83 (Illus. 16).[26]

THE MASSEY MANUFACTURING COMPANY OFFICE BUILDING

In March 1883 a reporter from the *Globe* wrote a story about the building-trade prospects for the coming season.[27] The writer had interviewed a number of prominent architects who, "having suffered through a strike and lost opportunities the previous season, believed it wise not to give out information about their prospects." The writer pointed out that W. Storm, one of Toronto's more successful architects, supported these sentiments because information pertaining to trade prospects "might strengthen the hands of those who were contemplating demanding increased wages." Only seven architects spoke frankly about their upcoming assignments. Lennox was at the top of the list with seventeen projects, followed by Langley, Langley, & Burke with eight. The remaining five firms accounted for thirty other prospective assignments. Two significant pieces of information about Lennox can be derived from the report. The first is that he had a very busy practice. The second is that he was not afraid of the threat of increasing wage demands and/or labour reprisal.

Two of Lennox's commissions highlighted in the article were offices for the Massey Manufacturing Company as well as a residence and coach-house on Jarvis Street for Charles H. Massey. Lennox started the office structure in 1883, and by 1885 the building was completed (Illus. 17).[28] A foursquare, red-brick building, very much in keeping with Queen Anne Revival style. It boasted bay windows, dormers, and a wonderful belvedere. Charles died in 1884 and did not live to see it completed. Nor did he live to see the completion of his house at 519 Jarvis Street.

The gabled, red-brick Queen Anne Revival–style house on Jarvis Street stayed in the family (it was bought by Charles's brother, H.A. Massey, for his son, Chester

Daniel Massey)[29] and is still standing. It has suffered from inept and unsympathetic additions, but Lennox's signature use of intricate brickwork and terracotta is still evident on the west elevation. A curved, leaded-glass stair-hall window, original to the house and exceptional in its execution, remains undamaged (Illus. 18). As with most of Lennox's residential designs, the main staircase starts at the south, rises to a landing, and is lit by an intricate window placed to receive light from the north.

LAILEY RESIDENCE AND 664–682 YONGE STREET

Lennox was also working on 280 Bloor Street West for William Lailey (Illus. 19).[30] His interpretation of the Queen Anne style was changing, and the structure was not as appealing as the Massey residence. The combination of a number of elements combined to create a less than coherent design. Corbelling like that featured in the turret of the Bloor Street Baptist Church bell tower was used here as a support for a window on the west side of the house. A polygonal tower with shingles, terracotta panelling, and sharply pointed roof completed the east side of the façade. Above the oriels and breaking the roof line was a balcony, resting on prominent brackets, the whole being surmounted by a weighty projecting gable. Another of his 1883 designs, the Scottish Ontario & Manitoba Land Company, at 664–682 Yonge Street,[31] shows that Lennox had not abandoned the Second Empire style (Illus. 20 and 21). This row of stores is much more forceful in appearance than any of its immediate neighbours.

THE MANNING ARCADE

By 1884 Alexander Manning, a Toronto real estate baron, had become one of Lennox's clients. For a number of years, Lennox had been one of Manning's tenants. In 1881, after having set up his practice, he had moved his offices to the Manning Block; now he became Manning's architect, and the first structure designed by Lennox for his new client was suitably called the "Manning Arcade"[32] (Illus. 22). Without question, it was inspired by another property owned by Manning, the Grand Opera House, 1879 (architect unknown; Illus. 23). The Arcade entrance was heavily ornamented, with caryatids holding up a pediment that announced the name of the building and an Atlas-like figure carrying an ornate balcony on his shoulders. Above the entrance, a deep recess was filled by a two-tiered oriel. The building sported all manner of decoration. Though an exercise in ostentation, it was regarded as a handsome and imposing structure in its time. Mayor of Toronto in 1885 and an important ratepayer,[33] Manning was to prove an important client and friend to Lennox, especially with regard to the competition for and the building of Toronto's municipal and county buildings.

VICTORIA HALL

From the ornate to the subtle: Lennox's next known building was the Victoria Hall on Queen Street East, for the Orange Association (Illus. 24).[34] When Eric Arthur, in his 1964 edition of *Toronto: No Mean City*, wrote, "We are only beginning to appreciate Lennox as an architect,"[35] it was this building that prompted the observation. Arthur admired the hall for its "charm" and its wonderful brickwork. In this work, Lennox managed to tie the elements together in a very neat package. The building was thought of as a piece of sculpture, with brickwork creating light and shade. Elegance and distinction were created by the crisp design of arcading and drop pilaster-strips.

THE BEATTY BUILDING

An office building constructed for William Henry Beatty circa 1885–86 was completely unlike the Victoria Hall.[36] Lennox looked to Europe for inspiration in creating the design for this rather small building at 3 King Street West (Illus. 25). He had many folio volumes on architecture, modern and old, publications from both sides of the Atlantic, to draw on for this exercise. It resembles the Manning Arcade in its excess if not in specific detail. Nearly every surface of the façade was embellished. If nothing else it was a conspicuous testimonial to the wealth of its owner, Beatty, whose bust surveyed the street from the apex of the building.

Three levels of pilasters defined the horizontal limits of the façade; each level was treated differently. The first set of pilasters was stylized and geometric. The second set was rusticated, fluted and topped by Ionic capitals. The third set was flat, but shouldered caryatids which in turn carried a heavy attic storey. Beatty's building was very much in keeping with contemporary European commercial buildings. By the time the Beatty Building was finished, Lennox was already at work competing for one of his most important commissions, and one of his most admired buildings, Toronto's "Old City Hall."

Tenders Wanted,

TENDERS.

The Western Counties Railway of Nova Scotia.

The undersigned invite tenders for the Superstructure of a

RAILWAY BRIDGE ACROSS THE SISSIBOO RIVER, AT WEYMOUTH, NOVA SCOTIA,

Consisting of nine spans 30 feet, nine spans 30 feet, and one draw span 50 feet. Further particulars will be forwarded on application personally or by letter to

SHANLY & PLUNKETT,
a   Chief Contractors W. C. Railway.

TO CARPENTER-BUILDERS.

Lump Tenders will be received until five o'clock p.m., THURSDAY, the 17th instant, for the several works required to be done in making additions to and general remodelling of a TWO-STORY BRICK RESIDENCE, No. 241, east side of Jarvis-street, Toronto. Lowest or any tender not necessarily accepted.
        STEWART & STRICKLAND,
            Architects,
4613   11 and 12 Masonic Buildings, Toronto-st.

TO BUILDERS.

TENDERS will be received until the 25th of May for the erection of

MASONIC BUILDINGS,

S.E. corner of Queen and Bathurst-streets.

Plans and specifications may be seen, and all other information obtained at the office of the undersigned.

McCAW & LENNOX, Architects,
    Imperial Buildings, 30 Adelaide-st. East.
The lowest or any tender not necessarily accepted.]
            6136

Illus. 5: Advertisement in the "Tenders Wanted" column, the *Globe*, 15 May 1876, for the Masonic building, Occident Hall.

Metropolitan Toronto Reference Library

Illus. 6: Occident Hall, 175 Bathurst Street, southeast corner of Queen and Bathurst streets, 1876, McCaw & Lennox.

City of Toronto Archives

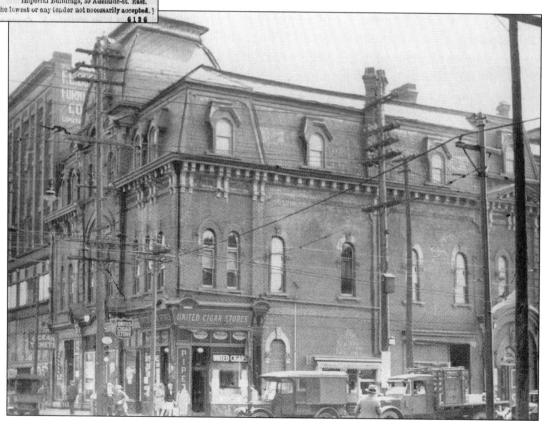

Illus. 8: Bond Street Congregational
Church. Monitor.

Toronto Historical Board

Illus. 7: Bond Street Congregational
Church, northeast corner of Bond and
Dundas streets, 1878, McCaw & Lennox
(demolished).

Metropolitan Toronto Reference Library

Illus. 9: Bond Street
Congregational
Church. Interior.

City of Toronto Archives

Illus. 10: Erskine Presbyterian Church, Simcoe Street, 1878, McCaw & Lennox (demolished).

City of Toronto Archives

Illus. 11: Sketch of Hotel Hanlan, 1879, McCaw & Lennox (demolished), from C.P. Mulvany's *Toronto Past and Present until 1882.*

Illus. 12: Hotel Hanlan, Toronto Island, 1879, as it looked in the 1890s.

City of Toronto Archives

Tenders Wanted.

TO BUILDERS.

Tenders will be received until
Wednesday, the 23rd Instant,

For the erection of three dwelling-houses
on Ontario-street.

Plans and specifications may be seen, on and after Monday next, at No. 6 Wellington-street West.

Tenders addressed to
W. A. WILKES,
64 Seaton-st., Toronto.

TO CONTRACTORS.

Tenders will be received until the 21st inst for the erection of a

BRICK VILLA RESIDENCE

on the Allan property, Shuter-street. Plans and specifications can be seen at my offices.

E. J. LENNOX, Architect,

Nos. 8 and 9 Manning Block,
South-east corner of King and Yonge streets.

Illus. 13: The first known record – advertisement in the "Tenders Wanted" column of the *Globe*, 12 November 1881 – showing that the firm of McCaw & Lennox had dissolved and E.J.Lennox was practising on his own.

Metropolitan Toronto Reference Library

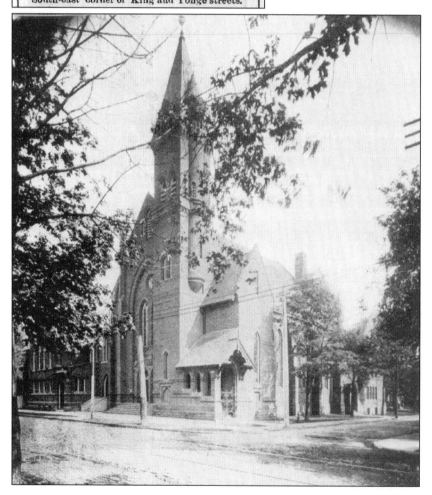

Illus. 14: Bloor Street Baptist Church, southeast corner of Bloor and North (now Bay) streets, 1882 (demolished).

City of Toronto Archives

Illus. 15: Semi-detached residences for Mrs. Bilton, Gerrard Street East, 1882–83 (demolished).

City of Toronto Archives

Illus. 16: The residence of H.E. Clarke, Esq., 603 Jarvis Street, 1882–83 (demolished).

Metropolitan Toronto Reference Library

Illus. 17: The Massey
Manufacturing Company,
701 King Street West, 1883.

City of Toronto Archives

Illus. 18: Residence of
Chester Massey,
519 Jarvis Street, 1883.
Interior detail.

Marilyn Litvak

Illus. 19: Residence of William Lailey, Esq., 280 Bloor Street West, 1883 (demolished).

City of Toronto Archives

Illus. 20: The Scottish Ontario & Manitoba Land Company, 664–682 Yonge Street, 1883.

John O'Brien

Illus. 21: Scottish Ontario & Manitoba Land Company, 1883. Detail.

John O'Brien

Illus. 22: The Manning Arcade, 22–28 King Street, 1883 (demolished).

City of Toronto Archives

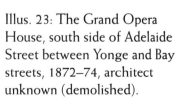

Illus. 23: The Grand Opera House, south side of Adelaide Street between Yonge and Bay streets, 1872–74, architect unknown (demolished).

Archives of Ontario

Illus. 24: Victoria Hall, Queen Street East,
1885 (demolished).

City of Toronto Archives

Illus. 25: The Beatty Building, 3 King Street West,
1886 (demolished).

City of Toronto Archives

2 Toronto's Third City Hall

The year 1886 marked a turning point in Lennox's career. He won the competition to design Toronto's new city hall (now treasured as the city's "Old City Hall"; Illus. 26), and for the next fifteen years, although he would be involved in many other projects, the City Hall was to be a continuing preoccupation.

Between 1884 and 1886, the city was in pursuit of a design for a new public building. What started out in 1884 as a competition for a county courthouse ended up as a second competition in 1886 for a combined courthouse and municipal building. A select number of the original entrants were invited to submit new or augmented plans, and Lennox, who was then thirty-two years old, emerged as the winner of the second competition.

To ensure his designs were not found "wanting" in any respect, Lennox travelled to "principle [sic] cities in the Eastern States."[1] In May of 1887 he wrote to the chairman of the Court House Committee that he intended to visit Buffalo, Pittsburgh, Washington, Philadelphia, New York, Boston and Albany. On his return he reported to the committee: "I find on the whole that my visit has been somewhat dissappointing [sic], that is, in seeing any building which is laid out superior or ventilated any better than the one which your Committee has seen fit to adopt."[2]

Lennox was being disingenuous: he was not "disappointed." It was his way of telling the building committee that he knew what he was doing and that his building could compete with what the best American architects had to offer. Much of his report was concerned with technical matters and layout rather than style,[3] and with good reason. In 1886 an American architect from Buffalo, Richard Waite, had been awarded the commission to build the Ontario Parliament Buildings. This action was considered devious and downright deceitful by Canadian architects. Waite had been part of the jury that found plans submitted by Canadians "wanting, more, it seems, for their handling of mechanical needs than for their overall conception, and design."[4] After the competition closed, Waite submitted plans of his own, and despite the fact that the projected cost of his plans was well above original budget limits, he was awarded the job. A great brouhaha ensued; Canadian architects were insulted and angry. Lennox's measured statement about his disappointment with the layout and ventilation in public buildings in large American cities was clearly intended as a rebuke to those Ontario government officials who were responsible for the fiasco.

In the same report, E.J. mentioned H.H. Richardson's Allegheny County Courthouse and Jail (1884–88): "Pittsburg [*sic*] is the only city of all the cities that has a building that is somewhat similar in its appointments to what your building will be." Lennox, like many of his contemporaries, was very much influenced by the American architect Henry Hobson Richardson (1838–86). Richardson, trained at the École des Beaux Arts in Paris from 1859 to 1862, is regarded as the pioneer of Romanesque Revival architecture in America. Nonetheless, he was not one to shun naturalistic High Victorian Gothic detailing: to wit, his Trinity Church in Boston, 1872, and Austin Hall, Harvard, 1881–83. Trinity Church in particular was highly influential and established him as an original and at the same time learned architect.[5] Lennox took to Richardson's early version of the Romanesque Revival and executed it in his own projects with great panache. However, it was Richardson's Allegheny County Courthouse in Pittsburgh, Pennsylvania (Illus. 27), that would prove to be of signal importance to Lennox.

E.J. indicated in his report that he had visited Boston, but made no mention of Trinity Church or Austin Hall at Harvard University. He may or may not have seen Trinity Church. And though he may or may not have visited Austin Hall, he did own a folio book, *Art for All and Decorations*,[6] in which the hall is featured. Lennox's columns in the front entrance of Toronto's Old City Hall bear a striking resemblance to Richardson's multiple-shaft and capital arrangement of Austin Hall.

By July of 1887, E.J.'s plans for the City Hall were complete (Illus. 28 and 29). The city council of 1888, realizing that costs would exceed approved funds, decided that it would have to put the matter before the city's ratepayers. The council also determined that an accurate account of expected expenditure was needed if the plan was to gain approval.[7] That spring, Lennox and the building committee, in search of materials appropriate for such an important building, "explored half the stone deposits of the province, travelled for miles in waggons over the most execrable roads to see out of the way rocks and boulders."[8] By July of 1888 Lennox was ready to advertise for tenders.[9] When tenders were in, costs were $582,034 more than the $1,050,000 originally stipulated. The total cost of the project was estimated at $1,632,034.[10]

In 1889 the city mounted a publicity campaign to convince its ratepayers that their money (including an extra $582,034) would be well spent on municipal and county buildings that would reflect Toronto's importance as a commercial and metropolitan centre.[11] The request for additional funding was approved, and work began almost immediately. The site had to be cleared of existing buildings, and the foundations laid.

Legend has it that E.J.'s brother, Charles David Lennox, was as much responsible for the design of Old City Hall as was E.J. himself. Without doubt their relationship was a close one, as Charles worked in his brother's shop for some thirty-four years, from 1880 until 1914, with the exception of two years away in New York City in the firm of Jardine & Jardine, 1885–86.[12] However, though Charles was an active member of the Toronto professional architectural community, none of the drawings, specifications, or letters connected with Old City Hall or any other project of Lennox's bear the signature Charles D. Lennox. If he was co-architect with his brother on the work, history has not recorded the fact.

At the "laying of the corner-stone" ceremonies in November of 1891, Lennox proclaimed that his building would "be second to none of its kind in America,"[13] but the building programme was to be fraught with problems and dissension.

As early as May of 1892 Lennox became dissatisfied with the contracting firm, Elliott & Neelon. He claimed they were using expensive out-of-town labour while Toronto was in the midst of a terrible recession. In a letter to the city building committee, E.J. objected in the strongest terms to this practice while "hundreds" of "starving workmen of Toronto … have to walk the streets looking for work."[14] In addition, E.J. complained of the firm's poor workmanship and substandard supplies, of rowdyism on site, and lack of progress. By 2 July he was warning the contractors they would be replaced if they did not immediately "supply a force of at least 100 stone-cutters, 30 bricklayers, and 60 labourers, together with the quality of materials specified in the contract."[15]

Letters and accusations between the architect and contractor flew back and forth. On 7 July Lennox reiterated the warning that if Elliott & Neelon's obligations were not met, he would have no alternative but to terminate the contract. But he added that, owing to his own "goodness of heart,"[16] he would give the contractors more time. By the end of August, Lennox's patience had worn out. He served Elliott & Neelon with a ten-day notice. Elliott & Neelon responded with a restraining order to keep Lennox from entering the site.

As the tenth day closed, Lennox decided to take action. Accompanied by a band of six policemen, he arrived at the site "while the echo of the midnight hour was still in the air," only to find all entrances barricaded. The police had been warned that the site was being protected by concealed armed guards. Nevertheless, Lennox scaled the fence and "dropped down into the enemy's ground." He was followed by the police. Once inside they found two "unarmed" watchmen, hired by Neelon, who refused to leave and had to be forcibly removed by the police. The site had been effectively stormed and retaken by Lennox. It was pronounced off limits to Elliott & Neelon, who then claimed breach of contract and sued the city. With Lennox as its expert witness, the city won.

After Elliott & Neelon were out of the picture, Lennox functioned as contractor as well as architect. Though he had helped the city fight off the lawsuit brought against it by Elliott & Neelon, his dedication and perfectionism were not fully appreciated by the city's building committee. As progress continued to be slow and costs mounted, relations between client and architect grew sharply discordant. Toward the end, Lennox was often called on to appear before the committee and to defend his actions.

It is an understatement to say that by the time Old City Hall was officially opened (1899), Lennox and the city councillors were not on harmonious terms. The councillors refused to allow him to have a plaque affixed to the building identifying him as its architect. Lennox, however, would not meekly accept such a rebuke: it is said that some of the grotesque faces woven into the fabric of the surface of City Hall are caricatures of councillors whom he particularly disliked. There was, as the council wished, no plaque, but "E.J. Lennox, Architect, 1889" was discreetly carved in stone beneath the cornice around the four sides of the building.

According to the building trade journal *The Canadian Architect and Builder*, Lennox's carved name was discovered by an enterprising journalist in 1899. A great public brouhaha ensued.[17] Though Lennox claimed he had not ordered the inscription, the journal came to his defence, citing European practice, even local precedent: "A prominent feature of the carving of the main façade of the Ontario Legislative Buildings, at Toronto, is a group of life size figures of the architect, Mr. Waite, the late Minister of Public Works, Mr. Fraser, and several of the other cabinet ministers."[18] In fact, Lennox did have his likeness carved in stone on the building, in the middle of a series of sculpted grotesques in the centre arch of the main entrance to the City Hall (Illus. 31). Not an inconspicuous position – but still one that a casual observer might overlook.

The disputes between Lennox and city council continued even after the building was finished. Lennox did not immediately provide the city with a detailed account of the amount owed him, but finally, in 1907, he submitted a minutely itemized bill for his services as architect and project supervisor, totalling $242,870.82, with a balance outstanding of $181,255.71.[19] Toronto's city fathers refused to pay, and Lennox sued the city. The case was taken all the way to the Supreme Court, but in the end, Lennox settled for the original sum of $65,000 plus interest, far less, he believed, than he rightfully deserved. "On Feb. 16, 1912, four years and one month after the writ of summons was issued, and 13 years after the City Hall opened for business, the case ended."[20]

The City Hall itself, the subject of so much conflict and litigation, is a massive square structure with a quadrangular courtyard in the centre. The west half, facing Terauley Street (now Bay), was used as county buildings, and the east half, facing James Street, contained the city offices. Each was provided with its own main entrance. The exterior of the building is rock-faced sandstone, built in a series of courses, relieved by carved bands and diaper work. The ground level is constructed of heavy courses of stone, cut to uniform height; stone work above the base line is random in height. Masonry above the roof line is executed in random ashlar work as well.

The key feature of the front elevation, its tower, was placed off centre, to line up with the middle of what was then the top of Bay Street. The tower stands on a base 10.7 metres (35 feet) wide and rises to a height of 79 metres (260 feet); roof and pinnacle comprise about 18 metres (60 feet). In the city's 1889 promotional brochure, the tower was described as the most striking feature of the main façade and as a reflection of the way the city wanted to be viewed: "It was designed to show solidity at the base and lower portions, from which it ascends with easy symmetry and graceful lines. The design is well relieved, and while conforming to the canons of quiet tastefulness, it is expressive of vigor and go."[21] A number of changes were made to the design of the tower between 1887 and 1899. The face of the clock grew considerably, so much so that it dominates the final product.

The requirement to locate the tower off centre posed no challenge for Lennox. He achieved asymmetrical balance through the repetition of pattern and measure. For example, a narrow circular tower, to the right of the main entrance, rises 10.7 metres above the roof line and reiterates the 10.7-metre base of the main tower. In addition, the east and west pavilions, though similar in shape, are quite different in detail. To underscore the drive toward asymmetrical balance, the east pavilion boasts a prominent double-storeyed oriel to counter the weight of the combined tower and west pavilion (Illus. 40).

This successful yet subtle balance makes the principal entrance the primary focus of the building. Closely grouped columns support triple arches. As suggested earlier, the organic and intricately carved capitals, where Lennox's face (Illus. 31) can still be seen among the gargoyles, were inspired by the ornamentation of Richardson's Austin Hall, Harvard (Illus. 32).

Inside the three large oak doorways, the centre one being 3.6 metres (12 feet) wide, are steps leading to a two-storeyed main hall (Illus. 33). Directly opposite are a grand staircase and an extraordinary stained-glass window designed by and made under the personal supervision of Robert McCausland, a well-known Toronto stained-glass artist. The "great" window depicts *The Union of Commerce and Industry*, and symbolizes the "upbuilding" of Toronto.[22] The stairway, more than 4.5 metres (15 feet) wide, leads to a landing from which stairs branch east and west to what used to be the county and city divisions of the building respectively (Illus. 34).

The main hall in its day was said to be the city's grandest indoor space, easily fulfilling its purpose of impressing visitors with the importance of Toronto. There were some minor critical quibbles: *Canadian Architect and Builder,* for example, did not hold the interiors in high regard. "Scagliola [faux marble] columns with plaster capitals are not worthy of the occasion; but their attempt to appear as marble is almost a merit beside the downright vulgarity of the woodwork – large grained oak or ash, slash cut, filled with dark filler and varnished to shine."[23]

Toronto's City Hall took more than eleven years to complete and its cost was $2.5 million. The cost overrun was staunchly defended during the opening ceremonies on 18 September 1899 by Toronto's Mayor John Shaw:

> Why people will spend large sums of money on great buildings opens up a field of thought. It may, however, be roughly answered that great buildings symbolize a people's deeds and aspirations. It has been said that, wherever a nation had a conscience and a mind, it recorded the evidence of its being in the highest products of this greatest of all arts. Where no such monuments are to be found, the mental and moral natures of the people have not been above the faculties of the beasts.[24]

Though the building celebrated its official opening in 1899, it was not yet fully completed. More than a year would pass before the bells in the clock tower rang out and the stone carvers finished their work.

In November of 1900 Lennox wrote a letter to the editor of *Canadian Architect and Builder* describing how he planned to have the three enormous bells hoisted to the top of the Municipal Building tower (Illus. 37 and 38). The largest of the three bells was 1.8 metres (6 feet) high, 2 metres in diameter, and weighed 5,443 kilograms (12,000 pounds). Lennox had devised an intricate plan involving a hoisting engine, temporary structures, and the like. It was successful and the bells were at long last heard, ringing out the first year of the new century.

Illus. 26: Old City Hall, 60 Queen Street West, 1887–99.

Metropolitan Toronto Reference Library

Illus. 27: Allegheny County Courthouse, Pittsburgh, 1884–88, H.H. Richardson.

Carnegie Library, Pittsburgh

Illus. 28: Old City Hall. Drawing of front elevation dated July 1887.

City of Toronto Archives

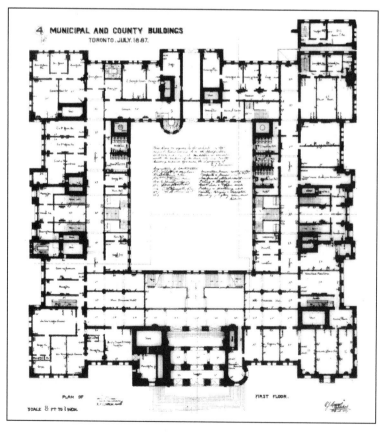

Illus. 29: Old City Hall. First floor plan dated July 1887.

City of Toronto Archives

Illus. 30: Old City Hall during construction.

City of Toronto Archives

Illus. 31: Old City Hall. Likeness of Lennox in capital of cluster columns in main entrance.

City of Toronto Archives

Illus. 32: Austin Hall, Harvard, 1881–83, H.H. Richardson. Detail.

Archives of Ontario

Illus. 33: Old City Hall. Interior main hall.

City of Toronto Archives

Illus. 34: Old City Hall. Main stairway.

Panda Associates

Illus. 35: Old City Hall. City Council Chambers.

Panda Associates

Illus. 36: Old City Hall. North stairwell.

City of Toronto Archives

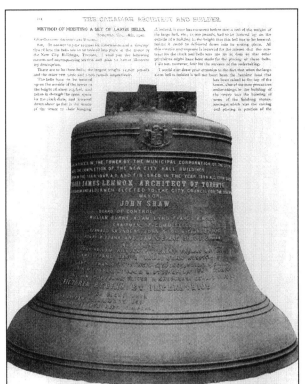

Illus. 37: Old City Hall. Letter to the editor of the *Canadian Architect and Builder* from E.J. Lennox, 18 November 1900, with photo of the largest of the three bells to be placed in the tower.

Metropolitan Toronto Reference Library

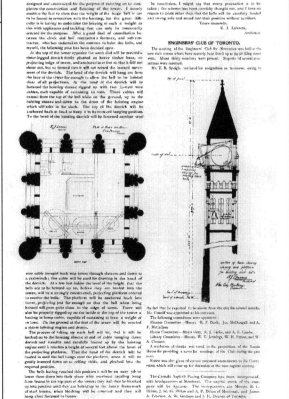

Illus. 38: Old City Hall. Plan and cross-section of tower and bells, November 1900.

Metropolitan Toronto Reference Library

Illus. 39: Old City Hall. Workers replacing the original red tile roofing with copper cladding.

Panda Associates

Illus. 40: Old City Hall. South and east elevations.

Panda Associates

3 The City Hall Years

MILBURN BUILDING

Though Toronto's City Hall occupied much of Lennox's time between 1886 and 1900, he still dealt with many other commissions. One of the more interesting of these is a block of five brick and cut-stone warehouses on Colborne Street, built for a Mr. T. Milburn in 1886 (Illus. 42).[1] Milburn, a wholesaler of patent medicines, occupied two shops; other tenants were purveyors of beer, wine, and liquor.[2] The building still exists and its detailing shows clearly that Lennox had turned to the Romanesque, and in particular H.H. Richardson's Romanesque Revival, even before he took his investigative tour of the eastern United States on behalf of the City of Toronto (Illus. 43 and 44).

Because the façade of the row of warehouses on Colborne Street faces north, deep sculptural treatment on the façade would have been wasted, given that the light comes from behind. Lennox created interest by articulating the façade in intricately patterned brickwork interrupted by rock-faced stonework. End and centre bays project slightly so that each unit is clearly delineated. At one time the centre bay was capped by a pediment. As with his row of shops on Yonge Street, Lennox used cast-iron columns between the load-bearing masonry walls to support large pieces of glass in the store-front windows. The Milburn building is one of the first structures to announce what was to become the defining style of Toronto.

THE ONTARIO MEDICAL COUNCIL BUILDING

Another important commission and another reminder that Lennox was one of Toronto's earliest and best interpreters of the Richardsonian Romanesque was the Ontario Medical Council building on the southeast corner of Bay and Richmond streets, 1886 (Illus. 45).[3] The design had the fierce and rugged substantiality for which City Hall would become renowned. Five storeys in height, the building was almost square. Its Bay Street front was 27 metres (88 feet) and its Richmond Street side 29 metres (95 feet). The first two storeys were built of brick and Credit Valley stone dressing, relieved with ornamental cut brick and cut sandstone panels. Red tiles (much favoured by Lennox) were used for roofing material and it was equipped with elevators and ventilated and heated by direct low-pressure steam.[4]

THE BROADWAY TABERNACLE

During this same period, Lennox was awarded a commission to design the new Spadina Avenue Methodist church. It was an award that came about because of one of his earlier designs. "On 29 July 1887 the Broadway congregation specifically resolved to build an entirely new church after the general plan of the Bond Street Congregational Church."[5] Construction of the church was begun in the fall of 1887 on the northeast corner of Spadina and College (Illus. 46).[6] Called the Broadway Tabernacle because Spadina north of College was unofficially referred to as "The Broadway," it was much larger than the Bond Street Congregational Church and was solidly rooted in "Modern" Romanesque. Lennox had, after all, just completed elevations for the City Hall.

Built of red brick, the Tabernacle stood on a base of heavily rusticated rock-faced granite. The entire building stood like a fortress on a battered base. The south and west elevations were dominated by gabled bays. A tower reminiscent of the one originally designed for Old City Hall served as an announcement for the point of entry to the church. Lennox tied the building to its base with two narrow granite string courses, virtually slicing the building in three and emphasizing horizontal thrust. The detailing of the brickwork alone was remarkable.

Lennox's love of fancy detailing was carried through to the auditorium (Illus. 47). The auditorium was quite large and accommodated a congregation of two thousand. But Lennox excelled at large theatrical spaces. As with the Bond Street Congregational Church, the rake of the mezzanine and the main level indicates his concern with sight-lines.

RESIDENTIAL COMMISSIONS, 1886–1889

When designing larger structures, Lennox was apparently much more rigorous about referencing discrete historic styles than he was when dealing with domestic architecture. By 1886 E.J. was combining the picturesque qualities of Queen Anne style and Romanesque Revival. One of Lennox's residences, 37 Madison Avenue, still exists and is considered to be the prototypical Annex house (Illus. 48). Though constructed in 1888, it was designed in 1886 for Lewis Lukes.[7] Lukes was one of the contractors involved in the building of Old City Hall.[8]

Despite the fact that it is now surrounded by many other like and new structures, the Lukes house remains one of the best designs in the neighbourhood. As Patricia McHugh commented in her book *Toronto Architecture,* "As a group, the [Annex] houses are impressive, but Lennox's example remains the standout."[9] Each level is clearly delineated, and each comprises smaller-scale and more intricate detail than the one below. The smooth brick arches of the front porch and the front window rest on rock-faced Credit Valley stone. Fancy basket-weave brickwork surrounding the arches yields to intricate fish-scale shingles on the second level. Latticework hides a shallow porch set into the gable end of the third level and echoes the basket-weave brickwork on the first level.

A house on Church Street, designed for Dr. G.R. Graham, 1888 (Illus. 49),[10] exhibits enormous inventiveness and control. From the tree-like terracotta decoration in its dormer to its basket-weave brickwork and plinth of stone, it demonstrates Lennox's mastery of design. For its day, it was highly sophisticated, even daring.

Not long after designing Dr. Graham's house and the rugged and showy Annex house for Lewis Lukes, Lennox designed 15 Selby Street, 1888,[11] for A.H. Rundle (Illus. 50). Similar in spirit to the Annex house, it is definitely more restrained. By 1889, 514 Jarvis Street was being built for Charles R. Rundle,[12] one of the leading contractors in Toronto (Illus. 51 and 52). Limited by a narrow corner lot, Lennox endowed this medium-size house with a great sense of importance. A tower serves to announce the location of the main entrance on the south side of the house. Rundle's residence, not unlike the house Lennox built for Lewis Lukes on Madison Avenue, is a successful alliance of Romanesque Revival and Queen Anne Revival ornamentation.[13]

FREEHOLD LOAN AND SAVINGS COMPANY BUILDING AND TORONTO ATHLETIC CLUB

E.J. could move with ease and vigour from the eclectic to the connected, but he was at his technical and flamboyant best in the head offices he built for the Freehold Loan and Savings Company in 1889–90[14] (Illus. 53 and 54). Shortly after excavation was begun for the Old City Hall, he gave his attention to planning this building. Located at the northeast corner of Adelaide and Victoria streets, the seven-storey structure was advertised as having two iron passenger elevators and private lavatories on all floors.[15] (While the boast about lavatories may seem absurd to the reader today, Toronto still had twelve thousand outdoor toilets as late as 1891.)[16] The exterior was Connecticut and New Brunswick brown stone and coloured brick. According to the *Canadian Architect and Builder*, the interior was constructed of iron framework and fireproof brick, so that entire partitions on any of the levels could be removed without affecting the walls of other floors.

The contrast between the Freehold Loan Building and Lennox's next major design, the Toronto Athletic Club, 1890[17] (Illus. 55), is striking. Where the Freehold Loan Building achieved grandeur by means of decorative brickwork, stone carving, pinnacles, finials, and variations on surface themes, the Athletic Club achieved monumentality through the organization of volume and mass. E.J. had been awarded the commission to design the lavish athletic quarters for a group of entrepreneurs. The building still stands on College Street, just west of University Avenue. It was equipped with Toronto's first indoor swimming pool,[18] a billiard room on the first level, several dining rooms and a whist room on the second level, and a gymnasium, more than 6 metres (20 feet) in height, that occupied the entire third and fourth levels.

While the tower of the Athletic Club echoes that of the Freehold building, it does not overshadow the roof line. The Athletic Club tower is connected to the upper two storeys, rather than sitting atop the roof line as in the Freehold Loan Building. Dormer windows break the roof line, as they do in the Freehold building, but in the Athletic Club they are less ornamented. Cross-axial balance was achieved by widening the base of the northwest and the southeast towers. This natural spreading of the base tied the building to the ground and gave it a sense of intense solidity and stability.

Balance was afforded the façade by the introduction of a terracotta panel into the blank wall to the left of the main entrance. The panel answers the staircase windows on the right. A tony look was imparted to the building by using expensive rock-faced stone for its foot-print and smooth granite for key components of the design.

A frieze over the arched openings in the entrance masks the dwarf wall of a recessed balcony (Illus. 56). Dark spaces created by the recessed gallery emphasize columns that comprise short fluted shafts and organic capitals. A lintel supported by the columns now carries the name "Stewart Building." It used to trumpet the name "Toronto Athletic Club." Unfortunately, the backers of the club ran into financial difficulty at the turn of the century. The building fell into the hands of the city and was occupied by many different tenants. As a result its interiors have been considerably changed. It is now owned by the Ontario College of Art. Fortunately, with the exception of the name and the front staircase, much of the exterior was left intact.

BOUSTEAD RESIDENCE

By 1891 Lennox was building a residence for James Boustead at 134 Bloor Street East (Illus. 57).[19] Like the Athletic Club, it shows that in Lennox's domestic architecture as well there was a move away from ornamentation and toward the organization of mass and shape as the source of expression. Here a look of importance was accomplished by the simple force of weight; the roof lay heavy on solid masses, and a prominent square tower dominated the east elevation. And even though some of the detailing is similar to C.R. Rundle's 514 Jarvis Street, there is an overall simplification in exposition.

THE BEARD BUILDING

Shortly after Boustead's residence was completed, Lennox was commissioned to build the Beard Building, 1892,[20] at the southeast corner of King and Jarvis streets (Illus. 58). It was a much-troubled assignment: planned as a nine-storey structure ("the city's first skyscraper"), it ended up being only seven storeys. Lennox's intentions were clearly outlined in the Canadian *Contract Record,* April 2, 1892.

> The building is to be a banking house and hotel combined, nine stories high, of Modern Romanesque architecture, to be executed in the form of an iron skeleton incased [*sic*] in brick walls, the exterior to be out of cut stone and pressed brick, the work of preparing the site will be commenced at once.[21]

When the building was being demolished, it was discovered that it had no steel in its fabric. Its joists and studding and beams and columns were of wood; its floors were bridges carried by brick walls as thick as 0.8 metres (32 inches). A newspaper item in 1935 announced the demolition of the Beard Building, which "has long been regarded ... as Lennox Folly."[22] Perhaps it was called a "folly" because it overshadowed its neighbours; it was the city's first and loneliest skyscraper. But as the article pointed out, if a skyscraper is defined as "a multi-storey building constructed on a steel skeleton,"[23] the Beard Building, with no metal frame, did not qualify.

If ever there was a building that showed Lennox looking for a new vocabulary, the Beard Building was it. Surfaces were almost devoid of ornamentation, and the slope of the roof and the narrow arcading set with V-shaped windows gave the building a skyward thrust. And the tower, though still very much a focal point, had become an integral part of the roof and attic storey. Despite the criticism it received, this building must have had special significance for Lennox: it was depicted in his personal bookplate (Illus. 59).

THE MASSEY MAUSOLEUM AND THE FRED VICTOR MISSION

While struggling through the Beard Building problems, Lennox was hired by Hart Massey to design a family mausoleum in Mount Pleasant Cemetery (Illus. 60). This little structure shows Lennox very much at ease with the Richardsonian Romanesque, capturing the essence of the style rather than its surface ornamentation. Solidity and solemnity were achieved through the use of impressive blocks of rock-faced granite and the organization of shapes. The sombre design is crowned by an imperious-looking female figure, right hand over heart, left hand holding an anchor. Lennox was very much in favour of having a figure atop the stepped pyramidal roof. In a letter to Hart Massey in December of 1892, Lennox indicated that his choice "would be a figure … but should you finally decide to have no figure, then my choice would be, as I stated above, No. 1."[24] No. 1 was an urn with flame and serpent entwined. Massey had complained to Lennox about delays in receiving sketches for the finish of the top of the mausoleum. Now, in the same letter, Lennox provided a number of excuses for the delay – among them, that he thought he would combine delivery of the designs of the mausoleum and "the new building on Jarvis Street."

The new building was the Fred Victor Mission, 1892–93 (Illus. 61), located at the southeast corner of Jarvis and Queen streets, and it was a staggering departure from all of Lennox's previous work. In a letter to Hart Massey dated 16 November 1892, Lennox stated, "You will note that I have only sent you plans of building; the elevations I have not yet finished. But the elevations I intend to make plain in appearance as I understand that you wish to keep down the cost as much as possible. Will send you the elevations as soon as I can get them completed."[25] Plain it was, but it was also decisively elegant and urbane.

Four storeys high, it was built of simple brick with minimal fancy brickwork; the basement level was differentiated by the use of deeply channelled granite. Its entrance was recessed into a northwest corner. The transition from angled corner entrance and recessed balcony above to a softer rounded corner was accomplished via the use of a cushion-like element. In this building the horizontal was emphasized. There was no tower, no hipped, red-tiled roof; instead there was a prominent classical entablature. Narrow bands delineating each storey rested beneath each level of windows and a garlanded oculus in the attic storey was reiterated on either side of the entrance way, again bringing the eye down. The proportions and rhythms were totally different from any of his previous work.

OTHER COMMISSIONS, 1890–1900

In addition to the Massey mausoleum, Fred Victor Mission, and the Beard Building, Lennox worked on many other projects during the 1890s. Among them were additions and renovations to existing structures, residential and otherwise (such as a new Sunday school for the Bloor Street Baptist Church and additions to the House of Industry on Elm Street); more substantial commissions were for the Comet Cycle Company and the Cobban Manufacturing Company. The first was a building on Temperance Street, completed in 1895[26] and later occupied by the Dunlop Tire Company; in 1905 it was modified again by Lennox for Aikenhead's Hardware Limited. Save detailing on the frieze of the entablature, the building is without ornamentation (Illus. 62).

The Cobban Manufacturing Company building on Lake Street was commissioned in 1896[27] (Lake Street was south of the Esplanade and no longer exists). Monumentality was achieved through the force of size and repetition of simple design elements (Illus. 63). Horizontal grouping was tripartite: base, shaft, and attic storey. Within vertical divisions, the windows diminished in size and increased in number by one with each progression to the next level of the tripartite design. This system of progressively smaller elements was used previously by Lennox, but never so severely.

The first two levels of the corner pavilion housed the main offices, in which the mathematical progression of design elements differed from the main body of the building. A single arch encompassed a triple set of two-storeyed windows, while the third and fourth storeys were defined by single windows set into a series of three narrow arcades. The fourth storey, just below the tower balcony, contained a series of four round-headed windows. The design was clear, clean, and distinguished-looking; it was after all the new headquarters of a company that said of itself "we are HEAD-QUARTERS for PLATE GLASS."

In the years from 1886 to the turn of the century Toronto's streetscape changed dramatically. Electricity began to be used to light the streets and power the previously horse-drawn streetcars. Many noteworthy buildings were being added to the city's inventory. Among those extant are W.G. Storm's Victoria College, 1889–92; S.R. Badgley's Massey Hall, 1893; D. Roberts Jr.'s Gooderham Building at Front and Wellington streets, 1892; R. Waite's Ontario Legislative Buildings, Queen's Park (officially opened 4 April 1893);[28] the firm of Burke and Horwood's Robert Simpson Company store at the southwest corner of Yonge and Queen streets, 1895; and J. Wilson's Holy Blossom Temple, Bond Street, 1895 (now St. George Greek Orthodox Church). Toronto's growth was sustained by a strong industrial base, and by the mid-1890s Toronto was on its way to becoming a "nearly national metropolis."[29]

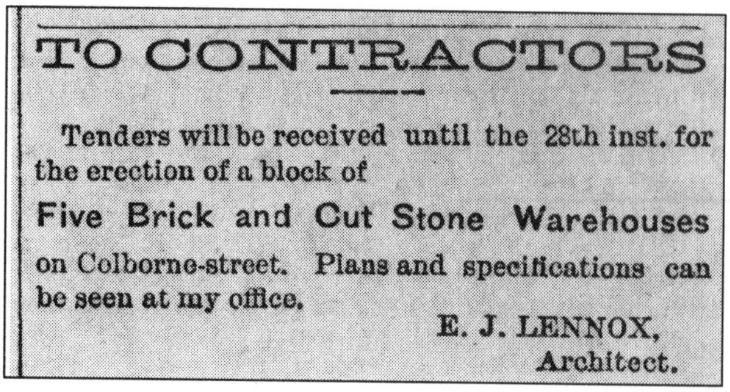

TO CONTRACTORS

Tenders will be received until the 28th inst. for the erection of a block of

Five Brick and Cut Stone Warehouses

on Colborne-street. Plans and specifications can be seen at my office.

E. J. LENNOX,
Architect.

Illus. 41: Advertisement in the "Tenders Wanted" column of the *Globe*, 19 June 1886, for the Milburn Building, 47–55 Colborne Street.

Metropolitan Toronto Reference Library

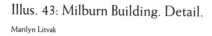

Illus. 42: Milburn Building, 47–55 Colborne Street, 1886. Front elevation.

Marilyn Litvak

Illus. 44: Milburn Building. Detail.

Marilyn Litvak

Illus. 43: Milburn Building. Detail.

Marilyn Litvak

Illus. 45: Medical Council Building, southeast corner of Bay and Richmond streets, 1886 (demolished).

City of Toronto Archives

Illus. 46: Broadway Tabernacle, northeast corner of Broadway (now Spadina) and College streets, 1887 (demolished).

City of Toronto Archives

Illus. 47: Broadway Tabernacle. Interior.

City of Toronto Archives

Illus. 48: Residence
of Lewis Lukes,
37 Madison Avenue,
1888.

Metropolitan Toronto Reference
Library

Illus. 49: Residence for Dr. G.R.
Graham, Church Street, 1888
(demolished).

Metropolitan Toronto Reference Library

Illus. 50: Residence for A.H. Rundle, 15 Selby Street, 1888.

City of Toronto Archives

Illus. 52: Residence for Charles R. Rundle. Detail.

Marilyn Litvak

Illus. 51: Residence built for Charles R. Rundle, 514 Jarvis Street, 1889–90.

Marilyn Litvak

Illus. 53: Freehold Loan and Savings Company, northwest corner of Adelaide and Victoria streets, 1889–90 (demolished).

Metropolitan Toronto Reference Library

Illus. 54: Freehold Loan and Savings Company. Drawing in the *Canadian Architect and Builder*, December 1889.

Metropolitan Toronto Reference Library

Illus. 55: The Toronto Athletic Club, 149 College Street, 1890.

John O'Brien

Illus. 56: The Toronto Athletic Club. Detail.

John O'Brien

Illus. 57: Residence for
Mr. James Boustead,
134 Bloor Street East,
1890 (demolished).

City of Toronto Archives

Illus. 58: Article in the *Evening Telegram*, 21 May
1935, announcing demolition of the Beard
Building, southeast corner of King and Jarvis
streets, 1892.

City of Toronto Archives

EX Libris

For the structure that we raise
Time is with material filled,
Our to-days and yesterdays
Are the blocks with which we build

E·J·LENNOX
· TORONTO ·

Illus. 59: Lennox's personal bookplate. Buildings seen through the portal are Manning Arcade, 1884; Old City Hall, 1889–99; the Freehold Loan and Savings Building, 1889–90; and the Beard Building, 1892.

City of Toronto Archives

Illus. 60: Massey Mausoleum, Mount Pleasant Cemetery, 1892.

Marilyn Litvak

Illus. 61: Fred Victor Mission, southeast corner of Jarvis and Queen streets, 1892 (demolished or concealed beneath layers of metal cladding).

City of Toronto Archives

Illus. 62: The Comet Cycle Company, 17–19 Temperance Street, 1894–95.

City of Toronto Archives

Illus. 63: Cobban Manufacturing Company, Lake Street, 1896 (demolished).

City of Toronto Archives

4 Palaces and Pantheons

MANNING CHAMBERS

As the new century dawned, Alexander Manning called on Lennox to design an office complex at the northwest corner of Queen and Terauley (now Bay) streets.[1] Manning Chambers (Illus. 64) shows that Lennox was aware of contemporary North American trends – a return to academic classical forms.

A number of noted architectural historians and architects[2] believe that the cause of modern North American architecture had been set back by the 1893 World Exhibition in Chicago. The fair "with its white plaster mirage of classical design decorated with equally academic figures so impressed a generation with its false grandeur that the advance of architecture was retarded for two or three decades."[3] Mainstream architects took to the vocabulary of academic classicism with zeal; it was for them a return to "good taste." Charles Follen McKim (1847–1909), an American architect trained at the Paris École des Beaux Arts, was the driving force behind the design of the 1893 exhibition.

E.J. Lennox was aware of but not a captive of these American trends. He adopted classical vocabulary, but continued to design from a foundation firmly rooted in picturesque eclecticism, intuition, and originality. Manning's office complex shows E.J. experimenting with a number of classical elements. Three sets of engaged Ionic columns framed doorways to a very shallow balustraded balcony over the main entrance, the attic storey was topped by a sharply defined entablature, and corner pavilions were accentuated by narrow, elongated rusticated quoins.

E.J. AND THE ARCHITECTURAL EIGHTEEN CLUB

The year following this assignment, in 1901, Lennox took part in the First Annual Exhibition of the Architectural Eighteen Club. The club was established in January of 1899 as an informal group whose chief aim was the promotion of fellowship among young architects. It had come into being partly in reaction to a revolt of sorts against the Ontario Association of Architects (OAA). Lennox, along with a number of younger members of the profession, distanced himself from the OAA after a pupil in E.J.'s office was refused entry to the association despite having successfully completed a required test. The student, a Mr. McCallum,

> entered suit against the O.A.A. to show cause why he had not been permitted to become a member. In the Court investigation it became evident that the successful candidates were not selected according to the marks attained, some with low marks being approved and some with high marks not. The Association's explanation to the Court was that some were younger men who could afford to take more years to qualify.[4]

The Eighteen Club later joined the Architectural League of America; the 1901 exhibition was mounted under the auspices of the league. "The exhibition of the league was the most important and perhaps the biggest show of architectural drawings held in Canada up to the time."[5] Among the Canadian exhibitors were such eminent architects as Henry Sproatt (1866–1934), Ernest Rolph (1871–1958), Eden Smith (1858–1949), Frank Darling (1850–1923), Edmund Burke (1850–1919), and John C.B. Horwood (1864–1938).[6] American exhibitors included Cass Gilbert (1859–1934), who would later design the Woolworth Building in New York, and the much-celebrated Frank Lloyd Wright (1869–1959). Lennox had on display a total of fourteen exhibits, among them a perspective of the Manning Chambers, a photograph of the Massey Mausoleum, a perspective of the Toronto Athletic Club, several photographs of the city buildings and a perspective of a proposed hotel for Toronto (Illus. 67).

THE KING EDWARD HOTEL

Lennox has often been given sole credit for the King Edward Hotel, 1900–1902 (Illus. 65).[7] However, a prominent Chicago architect, Henry Ives Cobb (1859–1931), created the original design. Legend has it that the idea of building a premier hotel at the corner of King and Victoria streets originated in the 1890s with Edward Aemilius Jarvis, a vigorous and imaginative investment banker.[8] Senator George Cox, head of Canada Life, and George H. Gooderham, head of the Bank of Toronto, took up the idea and as early as 1899 a permanent board of directors was appointed to "the new palace hotel project."[9] These men of means looked south of the border for architectural virtuosity. Cobb was one of those invited to submit designs, and his drawings were accepted. The directors placed an announcement in the *Globe* on Saturday, 7 July 1900, giving notice that "the construction of the Toronto hotel, a hostelry of the same class as the Windsor of Montreal and the Chateau Frontenac of Quebec, will be commenced shortly upon the plans now being drawn by Mr. Cobb, a prominent architect of the United States" (Illus. 66).

Though credit for the basic design rightfully belongs to Cobb, Lennox was awarded the commission, and he was responsible for the end product. Perhaps the backers were impressed by Lennox's proposed hotel for Toronto (Illus. 67) or the Palm Garden, 1899 (Illus. 68), at McConkey's Restaurant.[10] Plans for both had been displayed in the 1901 Architectural Eighteen Club exhibit.[11]

McConkey's Palm Garden was articulated in Corinthian columns that supported a barrel-vaulted ceiling. Mirrors, oculi, and a garlanded gallery contributed to its opulent appearance. Even after the King Edward had been completed, McConkey's was still the most favoured Toronto venue for important events,[12] and it was quite similar to the dining room Lennox designed for the King Edward. It may well be that the combination of McConkey's Palm Garden and the plans for Lennox's proposed hotel decided the issue; what is certain is that Lennox was asked to take over the hotel commission (working from Cobb's drawings). By 17 December 1901 Lennox was listed as the architect of record on the building permit; the cost of the building was estimated at $1 million.[13]

Much of the exterior design was clearly derived from Cobb's perspective, but if one compares Cobb's rendering with Lennox's (Illus. 69), it is easy to see that the original design was definitely amended and improved by Lennox. Where Cobb's design was polite, Lennox's was bold.

As planned by Cobb, the hotel was to have been only six storeys in "accordance with the latest ideas in hotel building, it having been found that guests will not take the risks of fire even in fireproof structures at great altitudes."[14] Less than four months after the permit was granted, Lennox was asked to add one storey to the mid-section and another to the attic level (Illus. 70).[15] It is E.J.'s attic storey that sets the hotel apart from its neighbours. Cartouches and pilasters (Illus. 71) executed in glazed architectural terracotta[16] provide the hotel with a sense of ceremony and differentiation that was lacking in Cobb's design; a change as simple as the addition of a porte-cochère to the King Street entrance gave it greater distinction. In its time the "King Eddie," as it came to be called, was the "first hotel in Toronto whose appearance befitted the status of the society and business clientele it hoped to attract."[17] Opened for business in 1903, it was an immediate success. "Its prestige was enhanced the following year when J. Pierpont Morgan of New York occupied its principal suite."[18]

The main foyer was designed to impress: giant columns supporting an open mezzanine are imposing, and the restaurant was, and remains, one of Toronto's most elegant and admired public interiors. "Modern architecture in Toronto has so far failed to produce a hotel dining room with anything like the flair and the gaiety of this one. The secret of the room's success is the decorative plaster work, which reflects credit on the designer and the craftsmen who executed it."[19]

RESIDENTIAL COMMISSIONS, 1901–1903

While Lennox was working on the King Edward, he was also designing a number of residences, among them the Rosedale residence of Hugh Munro at 69 South Drive, 1901;[20] 89 Elm Avenue, also in Rosedale, for C.R. Rundle, 1902;[21] and 234 St. George Street in the Annex, for Robert Watson, 1902–1903.[22] All are distinctly Edwardian (the Elm Avenue house, though still in existence, has been added to and much changed). Design elements of this house such as the octagonal tower, the roof sloping to the top level of the second-storey windows, and the curved and quoined gable are original to the design (Illus. 72).

Of the three residential structures, the Watson house on St. George Street is the fanciest (Illus. 73 and 74). Lennox proposed several versions to Watson, "the owner of a candy factory,"[23] and with each one, the plans grew more ambitious. In the end, the size (from original drawing to existing structure) doubled,[24] and with each edition Watson's home grew more decorative. The polygonal tower with sloping pagoda roof remained a constant throughout the design process.

A much grander undertaking was the house at 2354 Queen Street East, 1902–1903, for the noted lawyer D. Fasken (Illus. 75).[25] The portico of his residence is similar to one designed by Lennox for the shipping magnate Thomas Long. Lennox worked for Long from about 1890 until 1905,[26] renovating and adding to his house, "Woodlawn," at 513 Jarvis Street. A photograph of Woodlawn was presented at the Second Annual Exhibition of the Architectural Eighteen Club, 1902 (Illus. 76). Fasken must surely have admired the giant columns of Woodlawn because his residence boasted not single columns but paired giant columns supporting a much larger and more impressive pediment than the one at Woodlawn.

Expansion of the 1860s St. Paul's Anglican Church

In 1903 Lennox was involved in the expansion and alteration of St. Paul's Anglican Church on Bloor Street East. Designed by George K. and Edward Radford in 1858–60[27] and renovated by Grant Helliwell in 1890, St. Paul's was no longer large enough for its growing congregation, and the parish decided to renovate and increase the size of the structure. Lennox's expansion was faithful to the spirit of the original work: he lengthened the nave and added new transepts.[28] Lennox would later be commissioned to build an impressive cathedral-like church right next door. The 1860s church currently serves as St. Paul's administrative quarters.

The E.R. Wood Muskoka Residence

In that same year, 1903, Lennox designed, with meticulous attention, a shingle-style residence in Muskoka for E.R. Wood, head of Dominion Securities and manager of Central Canada Savings.[29] The design of the house[30] and boathouse is simple and relatively restrained for Lennox (Illus. 77 and 78) – a departure from his rather muscular city houses.

The Niagara Falls Palace of Power

E.R. Wood was a shareholder and director the Electrical Development Company of Ontario. Colonel Henry Mill Pellatt was its president,[31] and its office was at 23 Adelaide Street East, in the building Lennox had designed in 1889 for the Freehold Loan Company (by 1903 it was called the Home Life Building). Pellatt and his colleagues must have been impressed by Lennox's work, for very shortly after the company was formed in 1903 Lennox was commissioned to design the company's palaces of electricity – a powerhouse in Niagara Falls and a distribution station in Toronto. Construction of the enormous power-generating engines of the building was begun late in 1903, and at that time Lennox provided the company with preliminary sketches of the superstructure. Reasons behind his choice of style and material were outlined in a letter to Frederic Nicholls, vice-president:

> After due consideration I decided to adopt a classic form of architecture, therefore I have designed the building in the style of Italian Renaissance, believing this style of architecture to be one of the most adaptable to answer the purposes designated.
>
> ... In connection with the building, [I] might say that it is the intention generally speaking to build it of light granite, not to any unnecessary elaboration but to emphasize its beauty by pure architec-

tural lines and proportions so that when the building is completed it will have a characteristic appearance to answer the purpose for which it is intended, namely, a power house.[32]

Lennox's stated intention was to create a building "in the style of the Italian Renaissance," but he remained true to the resolute individualism of the nineteenth century. His approach to historicism set him apart from other traditional twentieth-century architects.

The design was approved by the Niagara Parks Commission on 4 January 1904,[33] and work on the power generators in Niagara Falls continued at a rapid pace. In the company's second annual report for the year ending 31 December 1904, Pellatt and Nicholls reported that "every engineering difficulty has been over-come, and that conditions, have, in the main, proved to be unexceptionally favourable."[34] Considering that the wheel pit is some 120 metres (400 feet) long and 45 metres (150 feet) deep, this was quite an accomplishment. The water passed through submerged arches into the inner fore-bay, then dropped down steel pen-stocks, about 3 metres (10 feet) in diameter, to the turbines.

The generators were well on their way to being operational on 8 May 1906 when the cornerstone was laid for the superstructure. Lennox (with handle-bar moustache and top hat) was captured for posterity in the commemorative photo-graph (Illus. 80). The harnessing of Niagara's power would prove to be a major con-tributor to the development of Ontario's wealth. Pellatt and his colleagues in the Electrical Development Company were fiercely nationalistic; it was not by chance that they selected a Canadian architect to design a monument to their enterprise.

The building is 27 metres (90 feet) deep, 12 metres (40 feet) high, and nearly 152 metres (500 feet) long (Illus. 81). Its façade is divided into five sections – the centre, two colonnaded loggias, and two end bays. Large windows behind a row of giant Ionic columns allow for public viewing of the machinery rooms inside (Illus. 82). The monumental central bay has a plain surface, a roof line that rises well above the level of the main roof, and an imposing portico that further enhances its importance and impressiveness. The north end is terminated by a semi-circular apse complemented by a pronounced entablature topped by finials in the shape of obelisks (Illus. 84).[35] Proportion, line, and material worked toward creating a dra-matic and romantic structure. Even the interiors radiated grandeur. The vestibule, rotunda in shape, was articulated in a variety of exotic marbles (Illus. 85).

While the powerhouse at Niagara was being built, Lennox was designing a transformer station at 451 Davenport Road in Toronto. The first known designs of the building are dated 1904 (Illus. 86).[36] The structure is an excellent example of early utility buildings. It now sits in great disrepair. Until recently it was partially hidden behind metal fence and all manner of modern debris (Illus. 88). Ontario Hydro is studying the possibility of an alternative use for this building.

When the Davenport transformer building was completed, it was said to be "the largest substation in point of capacity in the world."[37] Beginning on 21 November 1906, at 5:28 p.m., 451 Davenport served as Toronto's first point of electrical distribution for electricity from Niagara Falls.[38] Though the generators were up and running, the Niagara Falls Palace of Power would not be finished for another six years.

THE BANK OF TORONTO

During the summer of 1905, plans (Illus. 89, 90, and 91) were being prepared for the Bank of Toronto.[39] By November a building permit was issued and construction began. The building, at 205 Yonge Street (Illus. 92), has been described as one of Toronto's finest examples of Beaux-Arts architecture. However, it is more closely connected to European Beaux-Arts than to the excessive formalism dictated by American Beaux-Art architects such as Charles Follen McKim (1847–1900). The Bank of Toronto, like most of Lennox's work, was designed with an artist's intuitive sense of grandeur and drama, and with an innate understanding of the emotional effect of the sculptural. The building, for all its classically based vocabulary, is a powerful statement of Lennox's belief that individualism and symbolism should take precedence over restraint and propriety. The building is in many ways a theatrical set for the act of commerce.

By 1906 the building had reached the pediment. Elaborately embellished, it is constructed of Indiana limestone, which according to architects of the day was appropriate to classic design. A review in July 1906 criticized the design as being top-heavy.[40] The criticism was based on a drawing of the front elevation, and if one views the building straight on, rather than from street level, the observation may be correct. However, Lennox – ever mindful of his audience – knew that for the dome to be seen from the sidewalk below, it would have to ride high above the attic storey.

The dome, which is only attic space inside, is an architectural conceit. It is clad in sheet aluminum (Illus. 93), reportedly the first such application of this material in Toronto. A 1991 architectural conditions assessment judged the roof to be "in remarkably good condition" with "an estimated lifespan of 50 more years, unless mechanical or environmental conditions accelerate the present rate of deterioration."[41]

The Toronto Historical Board became the building's official occupant on 18 June 1993. Mayor June Rowlands, presiding over the ribbon-cutting ceremony, remarked that "this beautiful building, so painstakingly restored, provides us with a window to our city's past." She could not have picked more fitting words, given Lennox's importance to the history of Toronto's architecture. The extraordinary façade is intended to impress the beholder with its grandeur. Corinthian capitals, reminiscent of the Pantheon in Rome, surmount four giant fluted columns. Much of the surface is decorated. Festoons draw the eye to windows almost hidden under the portico, while wreaths frame bull's-eye windows in the attic storey. The frieze comprises an intricate pattern of palmettes and garlands, and a palmette sits at the apex of the pediment, while intricate ornamented blocks terminate the pediment.

As it progressed toward completion, the building went through a number of changes, but the main body remained the same: a four-storey U-shaped building surrounding a two-storey sky-lit banking hall. At first the bank was intended to serve as branch bank only, but this was soon amended, and it was redesigned to serve as bank and office building. Drawings indicate that additional land to the rear of the building was obtained only during the design process and that the plans were amended accordingly.

As D. Richardson wrote in 1973, "There is real ingenuity in the circulation pattern within the building, including the treatment of the second floor corridor as a mezzanine overlooking the banking hall."[42] Entrance to the main banking hall was gained through a narrow-throated, cross-vaulted corridor. Violet glass in the skylights and windows bathed the banking hall in a soft, reassuring wash of quiet light (Illus. 94). Floors were covered in a marble mosaic of half-inch white squares with a border of palmettes. The mosaic border echoes the interior frieze below the central skylight and the sculpted frieze on the façade.

Sir Henry Pellatt and Casa Loma

Even before Lennox began work on the Bank of Toronto project, he was having discussions with the charismatic Henry Mill Pellatt, who wanted a setting in which he could play host to royalty. Pellatt was affiliated with the Queen's Own Rifles and was fascinated by military history. In 1905 he was created a Knight Bachelor, possibly in recognition of his service to the Crown in taking the Queen's Own Rifles, at his own expense, to England in honour of the coronation of King Edward VII in 1902. Pellatt himself believed that knighthood was bestowed upon him for his efforts in the harnessing of the electrical power of Niagara for the province of Ontario. What is certain is that it was after his visit to England in 1902 that he decided to build a castle worthy of a Knight of the British Realm.

Between 1903 and 1905 Pellatt purchased some twenty-five lots east of Walmer Road on the edge of the escarpment and running down its slope to Davenport Road.[43] Only a hilltop setting would do for the castle Pellatt envisioned as reminiscent of medieval romances (Illus. 95).

When Lennox was asked to create a building that would rival the great castles of Europe, he took the commission very seriously. He and his wealthy client travelled

Europe and the British Isles in search of the perfect castle, the perfect detail, the perfect design. A preliminary sketch dated 1903, showing a design for the gates of the stables, indicates the extravagance that was to come (Illus. 97).[44]

Pellatt Lodge and Workmen's Cottages

Designs for the outbuildings were ready in 1905, by which time Pellatt had acquired title to the land. Pellatt Lodge was the first structure to be completed (Illus. 98). It is a two-storey residence built of red-brown brick with cast-stone trim. It still dominates the northwest corner of Walmer Road and Austin Terrace, just south of the Casa Loma stables. The south and east perimeters of the property are delineated by a low stone wall surmounted by a stone balustrade. Access to the house is at the southeast corner of the lot through an imposing set of gateposts. Octagonal towers with gently curving roofs punctuate the front elevation, and a hipped roof slopes to the first level, providing the building with a downward thrust. The cottages (two semi-detached homes in a single structure) that were designed for workmen echo the lodge in some of their elements. The building still stands north of the stables, and though it looks as though it was renovated in the 1950s, one can still see that it was originally designed to complement the stables and lodge (Illus. 99 and 100).[45]

The Stables

By 1906 the Casa Loma stables were under construction (Illus. 101). The structure is extraordinarily grand and can compete with the most lavish anywhere on the continent. Stalls are of mahogany; floors are covered in Spanish tiles laid in a herringbone pattern to prevent horses from slipping; and casement windows above the stalls are hinged at the bottom so as to open towards the ceiling and prevent the horses from being subjected to drafts. The main entrances are framed in white cast stone, differentiating them from the red-brick body of the building (Illus. 102). Adding further importance, finials in the form of heraldic beasts sit atop rusticated buttresses (Illus. 104); they were inspired by those at the entrance front of Hampton Court and Hengrave Hall, Suffolk (Illus. 105).[46] Another three years of intense research, dialogue, and design passed before shovel was put to ground for the building of Casa Loma. A permit to build the main house was granted to Col. Sir H.M. Pellatt on 16 December 1909.[47]

Designing a Castle

Casa Loma is certainly one of Canada's more formidable pieces of residential architecture. As W. Dendy and W. Kilbourn observed, "No Edwardian building in Toronto is more remarkable than Casa Loma, the largest house ever built in

Canada."[48] It was an enormous undertaking: plans comprised ninety-eight rooms, five thousand electric lights, an electrically operated elevator, a shooting gallery almost 50 metres (160 feet) long, a wine cellar, an indoor fountain, and a marble swimming pool. Lennox looked to medieval castles for design inspiration, but Casa Loma is much more in keeping with sixteenth- and seventeenth-century castles, which were no longer concerned with the realities of medieval warfare; their fortress-like appearance had become an architectural conceit, a symbol of a nobleman's dwelling.[49]

Lennox's concept of a romantic castle was impressively realized. The building is dominated by towers and a complicated skyline. White cast-stone battlements, chimneys, and corbelled towers pierce the sky; the highest of the towers, crowned by a conical roof, looks out over the city of Toronto. Varying points carry obelisk finials. A buttressed porte-cochère reiterates the shape of the square entrance tower (Illus. 106), softening the façade of the building and rendering it much less intimidating than its south-facing elevation. Down-spouts were buried, so as not to detract from the medieval illusion.

Lennox created an intensely individualistic statement, which exploited location to great dramatic effect. In the spirit of the Castle of Neuschwanstein, Bavaria, 1881, built for Ludwig II of Bavaria,[50] Casa Loma was built not for actual defence but to create an impression of impregnability. It stands as a reminder of the ostentatious display of wealth that was *de rigueur* in North America at the turn of the century.

Entrance is gained at ground level by way of the porte-cochère. The entry, a fairly short passageway, leads to a corridor that runs from the westerly part of the house to the conservatory on the east. Part of the corridor is directly beneath a gallery that overlooks the Great Hall. The corridor to the east of the entry, called "Peacock Alley" (Illus. 107), is panelled in oak, and its floor is constructed of reinforced concrete intended to support Pellatt's large collection of medieval and early Renaissance armour.[51]

The first of the main-level rooms a visitor to Casa Loma encounters is the Great Hall. It is an immense room with an exceptional hammer-beam roof and a 12-metre-high (40-foot) leaded-glass window comprising 738 lights. Each of the public rooms was designed to create a different atmosphere, with materials and style adding to the effect. Sir Henry's drawing room, the Oak Room, is elaborately panelled in the style of Grinling Gibbons (1648–1721), a famous English Renaissance carver whose ornate woodwork decorates many of England's country houses. The carving is said to have been done by Italian artisans brought to Toronto especially for the task. Indirect lighting, much like that used in the Palm Garden at McConkey's Restaurant, was used so as not to detract from the ornamented plaster ceiling. The billiard room and drawing rooms are on the west side of the house; the dining room and library are to the east of the Great Hall. The library is exceptionally large, with herring-bone hardwood flooring and an Elizabethan-style plasterwork ceiling. Bookcases capacious enough for many thousands of books line the walls. At the end of Peacock Alley enormous bronze-and-glass doors open to reveal an opulent conservatory. The doors were fitted so that the quarter-inch plate glass swings free on piano-hinges for ease of cleaning. The conservatory's special features include an elaborate stained-glass dome, leaded-glass windows, and a marble floor, dado, and fountain.

The second storey of the castle was the private domain of Sir Henry and Lady Pellatt. Each had their own set of rooms. Lady Pellatt's suite, some 278 square metres (3,000 square feet) in all, included a bedroom, sitting room, bathroom, and balcony overlooking the city and castle grounds. The plasterwork, in ceiling and walls, is delicate. Sir Henry's bedroom, approximately 18 by 12 metres (60 by 40 feet), is panelled in mahogany with pilasters, one of them fitted with a hidden compartment.

Fixtures and systems were state-of-the-art. Case Loma was equipped with a central vacuum system, a master electric-light system controlled from a panel in Sir Henry's bedroom, and a temperature-controlled wine cellar. A rifle range and marble swimming pool were planned but never completed. The complex included the castle, the stables (with a tunnel to the main house), a lodge, a greenhouse nearly half an acre in size, workmen's cottages, and extensive gardens. The gardens and greenhouse (Illus. 108) are gone.

Sir Henry intended to leave the castle to Toronto as a museum when he died. It cost him more than $3 million, quite an amount even for Edwardian times, though it pales in comparison with the $11 million the American Vanderbilt family spent on their summer cottage, Marble House, in Newport, Rhode Island, 1888, designed by Richard Hunt (1827–95).

The Pellatts did not move into their "spectacular house" until 1913, and even then it was far from finished. They lived with scaffolding and bunting in the Great Hall for many years.[52] The First World War impeded construction, and as late as 1916 Lennox was still providing Pellatt with drawings for items such as hardware. In fact, Pellatt was never able to complete Casa Loma, because of financial difficulties. He mortgaged his home against his investments, and when he went bankrupt he lost Casa Loma to the city for back taxes. His furnishings were ignobly auctioned off in 1924, and at the time of the sale Sir Henry told a *Toronto Star* reporter, "It is a sale which breaks my heart."[53]

Casa Loma has been ridiculed for its ostentation, and will in all likelihood continue to be, despite the fact it is one of the most visited tourism sites in Toronto. Since 1937 Casa Loma has been run by the Kiwanis Club and is open to the public as a means of raising funds for charitable works. The lodge is owned by the city but is not open to the public, and the workmen's cottages are now privately held.

Much had happened to the city in the years between the ringing of the bells in the clock tower of Old City Hall and the outbreak of the First World War. To its cultural inventory of buildings Toronto had added the Royal Alexandra Theatre, 260 King Street West, built in 1906-1907 by John M. Lyle (1872–1945). And through the bequest of Harriette Boulton Smith, The Grange, c. 1817–20, one of Toronto's most important historic sites, in 1911 became the property of the Art Museum of Toronto.[54] And buildings in the heart of the city were reaching skyward.

Illus. 64: Manning Chambers, northeast corner of Queen and Terauley (now Bay) streets, 1900 (demolished).

City of Toronto Archives

Illus. 65: The King Edward Hotel, King Street East, Henry Ives Cobb and E.J. Lennox, 1900–1902.

John O'Brien

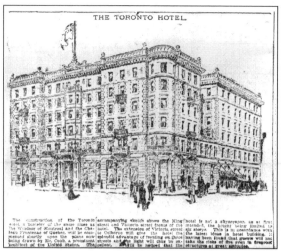

THE TORONTO HOTEL.

66: Announcement and drawing for proposed Toronto Hotel, the *Globe*, Toronto, July 7, 1900.

Metropolitan Toronto Reference Library

Illus. 67: Perspective of a proposed hotel for Toronto by E.J.Lennox exhibited at the First Annual Exhibition of the Toronto Architectural Eighteen Club, 1901.

Metropolitan Toronto Reference Library

Illus. 68: The Palm Garden at McConkey's Restaurant, King Street West, 1899 (demolished).

Metropolitan Toronto Reference Library

Illus. 69: Perspective of the King Edward Hotel, E.J.Lennox.

City of Toronto Archives

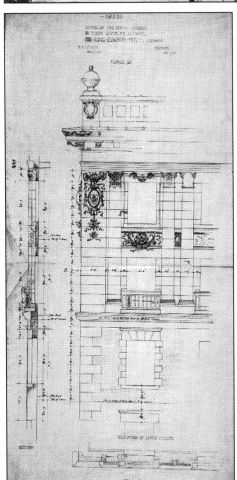

Illus. 70: King Edward Hotel. Drawing of upper two storeys, 1902.

Archives of Ontario

Illus. 71: King Edward Hotel. Upper two storeys.

John O'Brien

Illus. 72: Residence
for C.R. Rundle,
89 Elm Avenue, 1902.

City of Toronto Archives

Illus. 73: Residence for Robert Watson, 234
St. George Street, 1902–1903.

Marilyn Litvak

Illus. 74: Watson residence. Detail.

Marilyn Litvak

Illus. 75: Residence for D. Fasken, 2354 Queen's Avenue (Queen Street East near Balsam), 1902–1903 (demolished).

City of Toronto Archives

Illus. 76: Residence for Thomas Long, Esq., 513 Jarvis Street ("Woodlawn"), alteration to façade, c.1902 (demolished).

City of Toronto Archives

Illus. 77: Summer residence for Mr. E.R. Wood, Muskoka, 1903.

City of Toronto Archives

Illus. 78: Boathouse for Wood residence, Muskoka, 1903.

City of Toronto Archives

Illus. 79: Powerhouse for the Electrical Development Company of Ontario under construction.

Ontario Hydro Archives

Illus. 80: Laying of cornerstone of the powerhouse for the Electrical Development Company of Ontario, 8 May 1906. Lennox, in top hat, to the left of the cornerstone, Pellatt to the right.

Ontario Hydro Archives

Illus. 81: Powerhouse for the Electrical Development Company of Ontario, Niagara Falls, 1904–12.

Ontario Hydro Archives

Illus. 82: Powerhouse for the Electrical Development Company of Ontario. Detail of the west elevation.

Ontario Hydro Archives

Illus. 83: Powerhouse for the Electrical Development Company of Ontario. Main entrance.

Ontario Hydro Archives

Illus. 84: Powerhouse for the Electrical Development Company of Ontario. North elevation.

Ontario Hydro Archives

Illus. 85: Powerhouse for the
Electrical Development
Company of Ontario. Detail of
doorway in circular lobby.

Ontario Hydro Archives

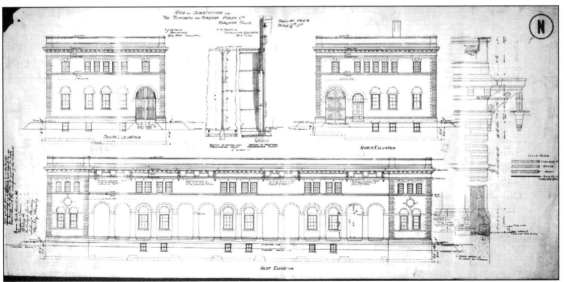

Illus. 86: Drawing for substation for the Toronto and Niagara Power Company, 451 Davenport
Road, Toronto, 1904.

Archives of Ontario

Illus. 87: Southeast elevation of the substation, 451 Davenport Road, Toronto, 1904.

Marilyn Litvak

Illus. 88: Northwest corner of the substation, 451 Davenport Road, Toronto, 1904.

Marilyn Litvak

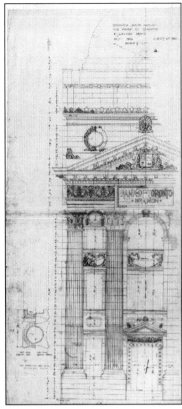

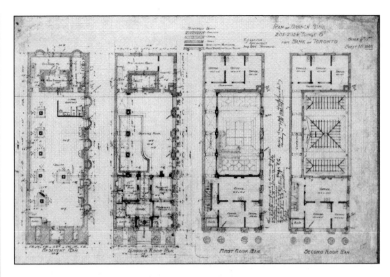

Illus. 90: Plan of the Bank of Toronto.

Archives of Ontario

Illus. 89: Drawing for the
Bank of Toronto, 205 Yonge
Street, 1905. Front elevation.

Archives of Ontario

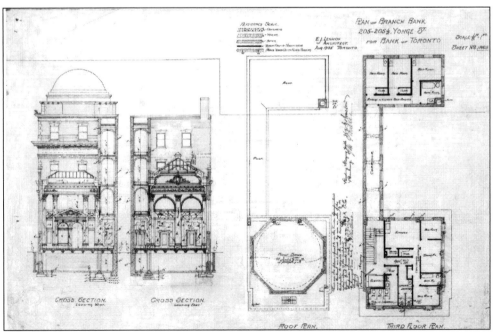

Illus. 91: Cross-section and plan of the Bank of Toronto.

Archives of Ontario

Illus. 93: Bank of Toronto. Detail.

John O'Brien

Illus. 92: Bank of Toronto,
205 Yonge Street, 1905.

John O'Brien

Illus. 94: Bank of Toronto. Banking hall.

Hamilton Public Library

Illus. 95: Casa Loma. South elevation.

City of Toronto Archives

Illus. 96: Casa Loma, 1 Austin Terrace, 1909–13.

Casa Loma Archives

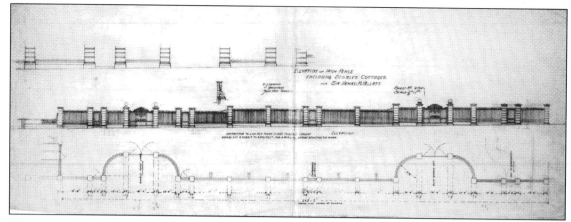

Illus. 97: Preliminary drawing of elevation of iron fence for the Casa Loma stables, 1903.

Archives of Ontario

Illus. 98: View of Pellatt Lodge, greenhouses, stables, and the gardens while Casa Loma was under construction.

City of Toronto Archives

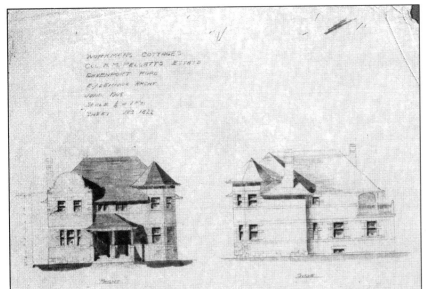

Illus. 99: Drawing for Casa Loma workmen's cottages, 1905.

Archives of Ontario

Illus. 100: Casa Loma workmen's cottages, 334 and 336 Walmer Road, 1905.

John O'Brien

Illus. 101: Casa Loma.
Drawing of scale details
for stables, 1906.

Archives of Ontario

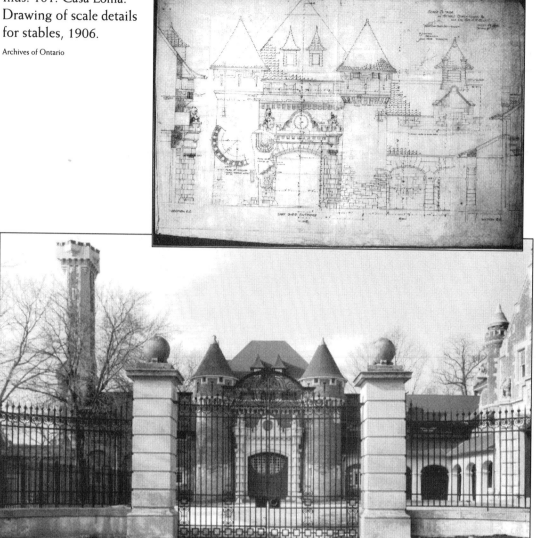

Illus. 102: Casa Loma stables, 330 Walmer Road, 1906–1909.

John O'Brien

Illus. 103: Casa Loma.
Drawing of stone posts
and iron fence for stables
and workmen's cottages,
1909.

Archives of Ontario

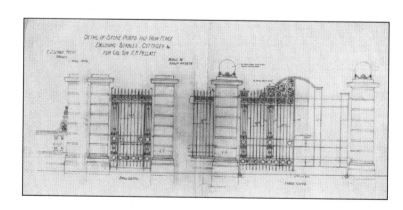

Illus. 104: Entrance to Casa Loma stables, 1906.

City of Toronto Archives

Illus. 105: Illustrations of heraldic beasts in T. Garner's, *Domestic Architecture in England During the Tudor Period*. The book was part of Lennox's personal library. Note pencil grid on the Hampton Court lion.

Archives of Ontario

Illus. 106: Entrance to Casa Loma.

Marilyn Litvak

Illus. 107: Casa Loma. Interior, Peacock Alley.

City of Toronto Archives

Illus. 108: Entrance to Casa Loma greenhouse, 1906–1909.

City of Toronto Archives

5 Last Works

THE WEST WING OF ONTARIO'S LEGISLATIVE BUILDINGS

While Lennox was deeply involved in plans and designs for Casa Loma, he was assigned yet another major task – the reconstruction of the west wing of Ontario's Legislative Buildings, Queen's Park. On 1 September 1909 it was badly damaged by fire. The structure, built in 1886–93, had been created by "that Buffalo architect" Richard Waite, and when it became necessary to rebuild, E.J. Lennox, Toronto's best-known and most successful practitioner of the Richardsonian Romanesque, was contacted immediately. Less than a month later, on 29 September 1909, he was advertising tenders for the "reconstruction of the portion of the Ontario Parliament Buildings recently destroyed by fire."[1]

Lennox was asked to increase the height of the west wing and the intermediate bay, and to render this section of the building generally fireproof.[2] As originally designed, Waite's west wing included a two-storey library at its southernmost end, lit by an enormous, two-storeyed, round-headed window. Lennox was asked to translate this section into two separate storeys. He did so, and modified the exterior to reflect the interior change. Although respecting the original design, Lennox changed the south façade of the west wing to more closely echo the south façade of the east wing (Illus. 109). Though the west wing was now higher, balance was maintained: the style and size of windows helped to create the illusion that the east and west wings were the same height. For the addition of a storey to the intermediate section between the centre pavilion and the west wing, Lennox again drew on Waite's original building, respecting the design of dormers in the east elevation of the east wing.

Given the task of constructing a fireproof structure, Lennox took liberties with the interior. He ignored Waite's wooden pillars and ornamentation. His west hall is different from the east hall in both style and materials, even though it conforms to the original floor plan (Illus. 110). The west hall is articulated in grey and white marble, in what was called "modern classic" style, in keeping with contemporary taste. Lennox's hall is cheerful and majestic; Waite's east hall, by comparison, is sombre and dignified. The difference is not simply a matter of the twenty-five years that separated the designs. A comparison of Lennox's interiors of Old City Hall, which were contemporaneous with Waite's east hall, indicates an entirely different approach.

WESTERN HOSPITAL

In March of 1909 it was reported in the *Contract Record* that Lennox's plans for one wing of the new Western Hospital (at Bathurst and Dundas streets) were about to be approved; estimates were to be invited "almost immediately."[3] The wing was to have been part of a larger H-shaped structure. In the end, only the west side of the "H" was built.

The main façade on Bathurst Street was an impressive 106 metres (350 feet) wide (Illus. 111). Built of red brick with cut-stone trimmings, the centre bay was differentiated by two towers and a base of smooth ashlar granite. A monumental staircase led to the main entrance. Simplicity in the design of the base, coupled with the method of masonry, served to convey the serious purpose of the facility. Lennox had combed through the history of English and European architecture in his research for Casa Loma, looking for the ideal detail, the ideal style for Pellatt's castle, and the results can be seen in this building. Elements belonging to Sir Christopher Wren (1632–1723) and Salamon de Brosse (1571–1626) were used by Lennox in the hospital's façade. Quoins on the end pavilions of the centre bay were derived from Wren's Hampton Court (built in 1690–96), while the attached square rusticated Ionic columns in the centre bay resemble de Brosse's entrance pavilion of the Luxembourg Palace in Paris (1615). Vestiges of the original structure can still be seen peeking out of the northwest side of an enveloping 1950s renovation.

There exists a letter from Lennox indicating that he wished his work for the project be accepted as a donation.[4] This was not to be the only occasion on which Lennox donated his services.

ST. PAUL'S ANGLICAN CHURCH

Some years earlier, Lennox had expanded the original 1860s St. Paul's Church. His redesign was carefully planned to harmonize with the existing style and period of the structure, and so in 1909 when the parish was ready to create an entirely new temple to God, Rector Cody looked to Lennox, who agreed but "insisted that his work be accepted as a contribution to the building fund."[5] The following appeared in the *Contract Record* on 17 March 1909:

> A new building is to be erected by St. Paul's church at an estimated cost of $150,000. The preliminary suggestions are for a building 85 x 175 feet, to be constructed of broken ashler [*sic*] stone and to have a capacity of 2,500. E.J. Lennox, architect has plans in hand and will submit a sketch of the proposed new building at the vestry meeting to be held on March 23rd.

The original drawings, dated June 1909, include a robust tower at the northeast corner of the church (Illus. 112), which would have had the effect of counterbalancing the horizontal nature of the 1860s church. Lennox always had the intuitive ability to factor in the totality of the picture and create non-axial balance. Though the tower was not built, Lennox tied the old and new churches together by using similar walling, of stones of irregular shapes and sizes. The failure to build the tower diminished Lennox's original concept (Illus. 113), but St. Paul's has a free-spirited quality akin to work of the renowned nineteenth-century English architect A.W.N. Pugin (1812–52).

Plans and perspectives were approved during the winter of 1909, and by 24 September 1910 the cornerstone was laid.[6] Three years later, on 30 November 1913, St. Paul's was "opened and dedicated for the worship of God."[7]

Three deeply recessed entrance doors and intricately executed tympana are surrounded by Early English mouldings. Above the doorways an arcade with pointed arches, supported on isolated columns, extends across the main front and side wing gables. Three large decorated windows above the arcade – sometimes called the "Three Sisters Gables"[8] – soar skyward (Illus. 114). Framed by cluster columns and mouldings, they are filled in with stone mullions and variegated stone tracery. Above these windows sits a stone-tracery balustrade, characteristic of cathedral fronts. Behind the balustrading rises the main gable. The design of the stone-tracery windows and balustrade is intricate in contrast to the simplicity of the main gable.

The apex of the gable rises 30 metres (97 feet) above sidewalk level. Stone-tracery pinnacles punctuate the gable, and buttresses emphasize the main section of the façade and provide horizontal thrust. Large transepts, extending approximately 10 metres (36 feet) on either side of the main body, complete the design emphatically, with each having an enormous rose window 12 metres (40 feet) high and 7.6 metres (25 feet) wide. In 1913 St. Paul's rose windows were considered to be among the largest rose windows in the world.[9]

The interior of St. Paul's is cathedral-like: the nave is 14 metres (46 feet) wide and 46 metres (152 feet) long, rising to a height of 28 metres (92 feet) (Illus. 115). The chancel, 14 metres wide, 14.6 metres long, and the same height as the nave, was enhanced by the addition of an ambulatory – a departure from contemporary Canadian church design.[10] The nave is articulated by stone cluster columns, Gothic arches and clerestory (Illus. 116). Transepts are the same height as the nave and are articulated in the same way. As with most of the work Lennox was doing at that time, precaution was taken to make the main floors fireproof: the oak pews rest on flagstones and the aisles are finished with red tiles. Lennox reserved marble for the chancel. The oak pulpit was designed and constructed in England. The building is lighted by chandeliers, augmented by concealed lights placed high up beside the organ lofts on both sides of the choir. Walls, finished in plain stucco-plaster, harmonize in colour with the stone arches and columns, while carved stone bosses and corbels throughout the nave and chancel represent angels. The plan was designed to allow two-thirds of the congregation to be within 21 metres (70 feet) of the pulpit (Illus. 119). Single side aisles become double aisles halfway to the pulpit. Robert McCausland, who created the windows in Old City Hall and the decorative glass in a number of Lennox's other notable buildings, also did the great chancel windows above the communion table.

St. Paul's was inspired by Gothic churches in England: its proportions are derived from Lincoln Cathedral, completed in 1192, and its clustered piers are similar to those found in the nave of St. Alban's Cathedral, Hertfordshire, build between 1088 and 1326. Lennox used the books he owned as a source of inspiration: for example, Raphael Brandon's *An Analysis of Gothick Architecture*, published in London in 1860, and Edmund Sharpe's *The Seven Periods of Church Architecture* (second edition, 1871). Some of them bear pencilled measurements and calculations.

THE WOLSELEY MOTOR CAR COMPANY

In 1913, while St. Paul's was being erected, Lennox was working on a commercial property for the Wolseley Motor Car Company (Illus. 120).[11] The building, located on Avenue Road just north of Yorkville and known for some time as the

Conservatory, was later demolished to make way for the expansion of Hazelton Lanes. Avenue Road was still fairly residential when Lennox was building this motor-car dealership, and he took great pains to use material sympathetic to the neighbouring houses. Though the structure was of concrete and iron construction to make it thoroughly fireproof, the exterior was clad in red brick and Indiana limestone.

The façade was divided into three sections: the centre and north sections were part of the showroom, while the south bay opened to the driveway entrance of the garage behind (Illus. 120). Maximum light and visibility were afforded the centre bay: each window was wider than the size of a car and as high as the lofty ceiling of the showroom. The entrance, showroom, and driveway were differentiated by strip pilasters that supported a tall, rather shallow cornice, but the main focus was always the showroom. A round-headed blank pediment complemented the centre section, lending it greater importance. It was a crisp design, and despite many layers of paint it remained one of the most interesting buildings in the area until its demolition in the 1970s.

POSTAL STATION "G"

One of Lennox's next-known commissions was Postal Station "G" at 765 Queen Street East, 1913 (Illus. 121). Again he was faced with a narrow lot and a corner entrance. A three-storey structure, it boasts a temple front on the Queen Street side and a colonnaded Saulter Street elevation complete with finials (Illus. 122) familiar from Casa Loma and Niagara Power House. It is a little building with grandiose pretensions; its giant Ionic columns dominate the area. The heavily colonnaded north and east sides overwhelm the main entrance. The covered corner door, topped by a balcony, seems to be an afterthought (Illus. 123).

Much of the interior has been changed. When the building served the community as a post office, the interior was quite lavish. Dados, counters, and consoles were all marble. Specifications were signed and dated "July of 1913," and on 22 July 1913 the contract to build was let; the completion date specified was to be within two years of acceptance of tender.

The structure functioned as a post office for sixty-one years. Prior to closing in 1975, it was designated as an historical site by the Toronto Historical Board. The "prominent landmark and focal point in the community"[12] remained vacant for almost five years and nearly perished. But the community came to its rescue, and Postal Station "G" now serves the community as a library-cum-community centre. Despite its lack of sympathy to its environment, it is a reminder of a time when federal buildings signalled the importance of public service.

LENWIL

In 1913 Lennox started to build his own house on the 2.5 acres he had purchased in 1905, at the same time Sir Henry Pellatt assembled his estate for Casa Loma.[13] "Lenwil" was completed in 1915 and still stands, minus some of its original property, just west of Casa Loma at 5 Austin Terrace (Illus. 124). The house is now occupied by a Ukrainian Roman Catholic order, the Sisters Servants of Mary Immaculate Christ the King.

Lennox was to live out his remaining years at Lenwil. After his death, in 1933, his wife, Emeline, stayed on. She died in 1935, and Edgar Edward Lennox (E.J.'s son) then lived in the house "for a year or two."[14] There was a period when it stood vacant, but in 1945 Lenwil was purchased for $28,000 by Frederick Morrow, the American "Nut King." Morrow wanted to alter the residence into an apartment house, but was denied permission. Lenwil was occupied by a number of families when the Sisters Servants of Mary Immaculate Christ the King were looking to buy a property in Toronto. The year was 1949 and Morrow sold Lenwil to the sisters for $55,000. The sisters' purchase of the house was fortunate: they restored it to a single dwelling, and for nearly half a century have maintained and preserved it, even to retaining Lennox family names on an intercom system.

Lenwil is a remarkable contrast to the ostentatious Casa Loma. It hugs the brow of the hill on which it stands. The roof, covered in one of Lennox's favourite roofing materials, terracotta tiles, provides horizontal thrust (Illus. 125). There are no turrets, no battlements; simple lines and clever massing combine to create a handsome structure of rubble stonework and stucco. Smooth granite was reserved for trim. The house is two-and-a-half-storey mansion, 30 metres (100 feet) wide and 18 metres (60 feet) deep, constructed of structural steel, stone, and brick. Servants' quarters radiate off the west side at an obtuse angle, affecting visual continuity between house and garage complex. The main focus of the façade is the central bay, which projects from the façade. Attached to the central bay is a porte-cochère which was at one time softened by a reflecting pool, complete with fountain, directly in front of it. The porte-cochère hides non-axial double doors, and an oriel window perched above its roof allows light to fall on the staircase within. Both the first and second levels of the central bay are clad in stone, whereas stucco was applied to the second level on the rest of the façade.

The house comprises twenty-one rooms in all. Double doors yield to a vestibule where Lennox, true to his proclivity for the latest in architectural technology, installed a row of buttons to control all electric lighting in the house and on the grounds. And as with Casa Loma, electrical wiring was encased in conduits. The vestibule opens to a magnificent central reception hall extending two storeys upward and receiving north light from a two-storeyed leaded window some 7 metres (24 feet) high. The reception area boasts the most exotic feature of the dwelling: an extraordinary cast-stone fireplace (Illus. 126). The chimney piece rises beyond the second level and is surmounted by an ornate pediment, its corners completed by Lennox's signature obelisk finials. A likeness of Lennox is carved into one of the capitals, and the initials EJL on a scrolled crest sit amidst a frieze beneath an exaggerated mantel. Each element of the chimney surround was lengthened so that the mantel shelf lines up with the floor of the second level. A window, providing a view of the reception area, juts out from the chimney breast and from below is almost hidden by the pediment.

Just behind the reception room and through a series of arches is a passageway that resembles Peacock Alley in Casa Loma, though of course it is much smaller and not intended to be a ceremonial avenue (Illus. 127). Principal rooms behind the passageway all face south – the library to the east, the drawing room left of centre, and the dining room to the west. Lennox's study was adjacent to the reception hall.

Bedrooms are on the second level. The master suite, occupied by E.J. and his wife, looks east to Casa Loma; some believe it was so that Lennox could wake and see one of the mightiest of his works. However, it was not uncommon to locate "best" bedrooms on the southeast side of a house, where they would receive the morning light. Additional bedrooms opened to a balcony above a loggia at the back of the house. The third level was reserved for billiards.

Attention to detail was apparent throughout the house. Elizabethan fretwork design in the stair rail and gallery is repeated in radiator covers and again as strapwork in the lintel over the fireplace. Most of the rooms are embellished with decorative plasterwork, and the ceiling in the drawing room is particularly noteworthy (Illus. 128).

McConkey's Restaurant on Queen Street West

While Lenwil was being constructed, Lennox was called upon by one his early clients, a Mr. McConkey, to build a new restaurant at 33–37 Queen Street West.[15] Completed in 1914 (Illus. 129), it was designed to carry another eleven storeys to be built at a later date, but the city never gave McConkey permission to build the additional storeys. Most of the exterior was faced in green-and-white, matte-glazed terracotta. Green marble was reserved for the pedestals of the large pilasters. The elaborately decorated entrance hall opened directly onto the main restaurant, and a dramatic marble staircase in the hall led to a second level. The first level was luxuriously furnished with "one hundred and sixty special chairs with wide service arms."[16] Walls were clad to a height of 1.5 metres (5 feet) in marble dado interrupted every 3 metres (10 feet) by marble pilasters that supported a heavily beamed ceiling. The ceiling was covered by dull white tiling laid in a herring-bone pattern. The second level, panelled in fumed oak to create a sedate ambience, could accommodate another 185 customers.

THE EXCELSIOR LIFE INSURANCE BUILDING

Concurrent with the building of the new restaurant for McConkey, Lennox was engaged in another project – an eleven-storey commercial structure for the Excelsior Life Insurance Company at the southwest corner of Toronto and Adelaide streets. It was to be articulated in the same modern-classic idiom as the interior of the west wing of the Ontario Legislative Buildings; sketches were presented for approval in April 1914 (Illus. 130). Lennox relied on the same system he used in the King Edward Hotel – a tripartite system of "pedestal, shaft and frieze"[17] with a transitional element between entrance level and shaft (Illus. 131). The whole of the building was surmounted by a balustraded parapet, which no longer exists; its absence has the effect of bringing the whole of the design to an abrupt halt (Illus. 132).

Though very much in keeping with traditional architecture, this building is endowed with a highly original two-storey attic. Florid Corinthian engaged columns and coupled pilasters at the corners provide the building with a rich appearance. Arcaded windows in the upper storeys are set well back from the shaft. Mouldings in the shaft were intended to be repeated in the transitional level but were abandoned to cut costs; cartouches and intricate detailing were dispensed with as well.

While most of the building is white enamel terracotta, the first two storeys are granite. The promotional material boasted that it was constructed with skyscraper technology: "The building throughout is lighted by exterior windows, thus insuring the best of ventilation. There are no dark courts, borrowed lights, or waste space. The partitions of the offices are sound proof." By May of 1915 interior work was well on its way to being finished. The total cost was estimated at $500,000.[18]

Excelsior Life is the last-known major building Lennox completed. In 1916 the building was featured in *Construction*, which described it as "one of the finest of Toronto's many high-class office buildings."[19] The following year, Lennox effectively closed down his practice.

Illus. 109: Provincial Parliament Buildings, Queen's Park, 1886–93, R. Waite. West wing and intermediate bay reconstructed and remodelled by E.J. Lennox after being damaged by fire in 1909.

John O'Brien

Illus. 110: Provincial Parliament Building. Interior, west hall.

Ontario Legislative Offices

Illus. 111: Western Hospital, northeast corner of Bathurst and Dundas streets, 1909 (buried beneath many additions).

Archives of Ontario

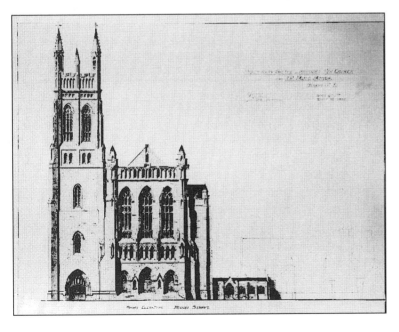

Illus. 112: Preliminary perspective for St. Paul's Anglican Church.

Archives of Ontario

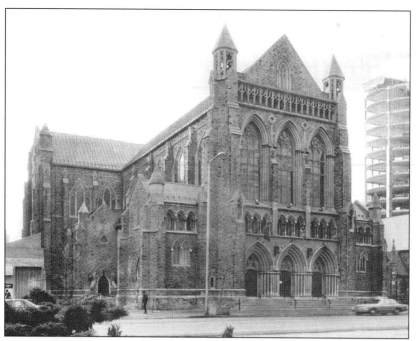

Illus. 113: St. Paul's
Anglican Church,
227 Bloor Street East,
1909–13.

John O'Brien

Illus. 114: St. Paul's Anglican Church.
The Three Sisters Gables.

John O'Brien

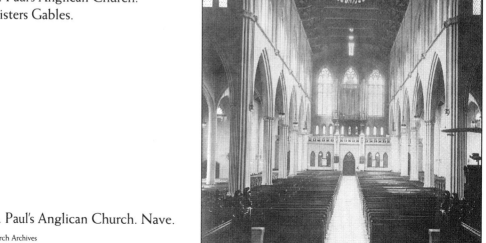

Illus. 115: St. Paul's Anglican Church. Nave.

St. Paul's Anglican Church Archives

Illus. 116: St. Paul's Anglican Church. Interior.

St. Paul's Anglican Church Archives

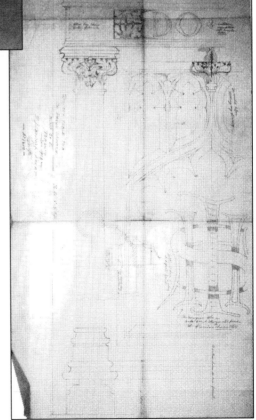

Illus. 117: St. Paul's Anglican Church. Sketch for chancel table.

Archives of Ontario

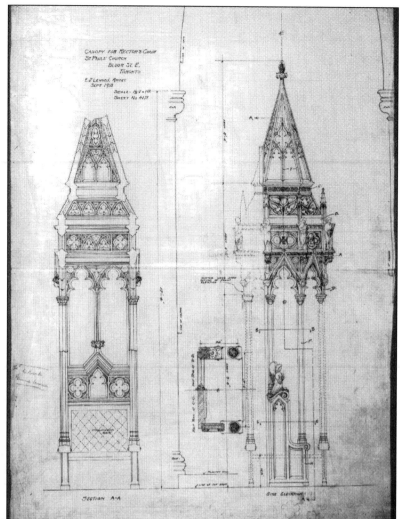

Illus. 118: St. Paul's Anglican Church. Drawing of canopy of rector's chair, 1913.

Archives of Ontario

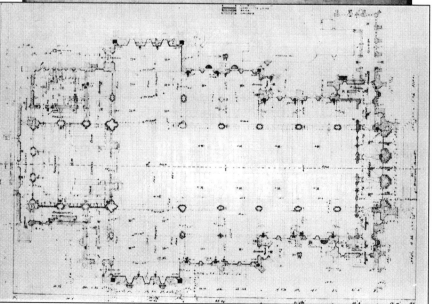

Illus. 119: St. Paul's Anglican Church. Floor plan.

Archives of Ontario

Illus. 120: Wolseley Motor Car Company, 77 Avenue Road, 1913 (demolished).

Toronto Historical Board

Illus. 122: Postal Station "G." Detail of finials.

Marilyn Litvak

Illus. 121: Postal Station "G," 765 Queen Street East, 1913.

Marilyn Litvak

Illus. 123: Postal Station "G." Front entrance.

Marilyn Litvak

Illus. 124: Lenwil, residence of E.J.Lennox, 5 Austin Terrace, 1913.

John O'Brien

Illus. 125: Lenwil. Oriel and tiled roof over porte-cochère.

John O'Brien

Illus. 126: Lenwil. Reception hall.

John O'Brien

Illus. 127: Lenwil. Corridor behind
reception hall.

John O'Brien

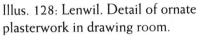
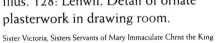

Illus. 128: Lenwil. Detail of ornate
plasterwork in drawing room.

Sister Victoria, Sisters Servants of Mary Immaculate Christ the King

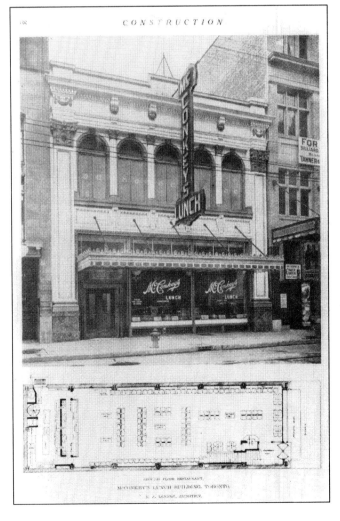

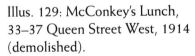

Illus. 129: McConkey's Lunch,
33–37 Queen Street West, 1914
(demolished).

Metropolitan Toronto Reference Library

Illus. 132: Excelsior Life Insurance Building. Corner detail showing upper two storeys.

John O'Brien

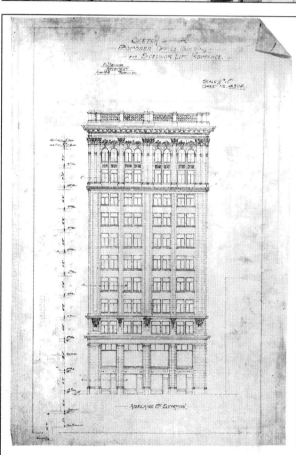

Illus. 130: Drawing for Excelsior Life Insurance Building, 1914.

Archives of Ontario

Illus. 131: Excelsior Life Insurance Building, 36 Toronto Street, 1914.

John O'Brien

Illus. 133: Offices of E.J. Lennox, 164 Bay Street (later 364), façade, 1901 (demolished).

City of Toronto Archives

Postscript

"TORONTO IN THE YEAR 2004 A.D."

Though E.J. Lennox's actions spoke volumes and his practice flourished, the only writing he is known to have done concerning his profession is an essay published in 1904 in *Toronto's Christmas Magazine* (a fund-raising project put together to benefit the Toronto General Hospital). In the article, entitled "What will the Architectural Appearance of Toronto be in the Year 2004 A.D.?" (reproduced in Appendix A), E.J. predicted that the coming age would be one of great towers and that the label "Architectural Skyscraper Age" would be viewed as a misnomer. When the year 2004 A.D. had come upon us, he said, we would look back and call this period of architectural history "The Great Tower Age." For Lennox, the concept of a tower age had symbolic overtones. Towers would serve as signals, beacons, points of orientation. They would be "towering buildings whose commanding appearance and beauty of design would be admired by all who saw them." Lennox visualized inter-building travel being conducted via "steel enclosed bridgeways," equipped with "noiseless tramway cars ... so that those who do business in the buildings would be transported from one to the other with the greatest possible despatch."

In general, the short treatise gives some interesting insights into Lennox's views: he saw himself as an artist first and foremost; he envied architects of the past, who he believed had greater freedom when dealing with clients; and he held in contempt communities that cared little about whether they hired proper architects or charlatans. In particular, E.J. predicted that by the year 2004 Toronto would have become a great metropolis, with grand avenues, lake-front promenades, and extended and widened commercial streets boasting tall buildings with towers set back to ensure occupants had "plenty of light and air." He also envisioned a vastly improved Yonge Street. E.J., apparently aware of French town planning and the Paris of Baron Georges-Eugène Haussmann (1809–91), had great hopes for the Toronto he helped to build. To that end, he recommended the appointment of a Board of Expert Commissioners, "whose duty it would be to see that no building would be erected except if it were of good design and would enhance the architectural appearance of the city." However, Lennox's words were not heeded – hence the architectural pastiche that is present-day Toronto.

APPENDIX A

What will the Architectural Appearance of Toronto be in the Year 2004 A.D.?

By E.J. Lennox, Architect.

In this age of commercial strife, when the human race sets up money as their god, is it any wonder that the professional architect, when asked to bend architectural forms and comply with every man's wish, has to stand aghast and think, or bow to this inevitable ruler? How different in the past, it would seem, must have been the order of the day for architecture, when kings' or men's whims had to give way and in place comply with what good forms of architecture would allow.

In the next age that is to come, when the next hundred years have rolled by and the twentieth century has ended, the question is "What will be the demand upon the architecture of that day?" It certainly is a guess to predict, and I can only assume what may be expected from my professional brother architects at that time. If I am to be guided by my own experience, I may be pardoned if I assume to state what the appearance of Toronto will be, architecturally, in the year 2004. If I am to come to my conclusion and judge from the demands that are made at present upon my profession, and enlarge my imagination in proportion to what the requirements may be a hundred years hence, I must take into consideration the ever-increasing commercial demands of the present day caused by competition in all walks of life. When one sees a community willing to order that the profession of architecture shall comply with their wishes at every stage, irrespective of the result; that they are ready to intrust the responsibility of erecting their buildings to the cheapest bidder, irrespective of their knowledge or experience, when we know how indifferent a thoughtless community is as to whether their buildings are intrusted in the hands of a practical architect, or handed over to one who assumes the roll of this profession and parades the streets with the name of architect blazoned upon his drays as a public notice of his ability, and in open competition to the reputable architect.

In the face of these facts, is it not taking a risk upon myself in predicting what the architectural appearance of Toronto will be in the year 2004? The nineteenth century has just passed. To this age belongs the credit, "if such it is," of the introduction of the class of buildings commonly named "skyscrapers," which is a misnomer and assumed only as a ready way to impress the mind with the loftiness of their appearance. Then if this name is to be applied to a class of buildings that have taken a leading architectural part in the nineteenth century, may it not, at least for the purpose of this article, be justly termed the Architectural Sky-scraper Age? In a hundred years hence, what class of buildings will be erected no doubt some of us at least would like to know. The twentieth century has now started in upon us, and its years that are numbering by, and when

Note: This article by E.J. Lennox was printed in *Toronto's Christmas Magazine,* 15 December 1904.

the two thousand and fourth year has rolled around, tremendous changes will have taken place, and as the requirements for all kinds of buildings are to be met, it may be surmised that possibly those that live in the future century will not be any more merciful to the profession than those that have lived in the immediate past century, and that Architecture may have to lend itself to meet the requirements and fit in with the moving of the times. What name may then be applied to the architecture of the twentieth century? It will all depend on the advanced or otherwise architectural appearance of the buildings at that time. It may be said that the architectural appearance of a nation's buildings is a fair way to judge of its education and its advance, or otherwise, position among the nations of the world.

Toronto is now in its early period of growth and advancing at a rapid rate of progress, which indicates that when the time has arrived of a hundred years hence, that millions of souls will be inhabitants of the future city of Toronto, and will all have to be provided for. The city by that time will have grown to such proportions that extra provision will have to be made to house its inhabitants, both in a business and home capacity, the accommodation for the traffic of both pedestrian and vehicle will have to be increased, and advantage will be taken of every available space for the purpose of safety and speed. The boundary lines of Toronto will be extended many miles beyond its present limits, all of which will have a great bearing on the architecture of the future.

Toronto in the year 2004 will be a great city reconstructed on new lines. The old city will be wiped out and a new city will be built up, laid out on a grander scheme. Special city laws will be enacted appointing boards of expert commissioners, whose duty it will be to see that no building is allowed to be erected except when it is strictly of good design and one that will enhance the architectural appearance of the city.

It is my opinion that at that time the people will be so sensitive to the beautiful that they shall allow more freedom and as in the past, the responsibility of designing and erecting of the buildings will be left to their architects, who will be selected on account of their reputable standing, and whose aim will be to study out the requirements of their client and fit them into architectural forms that will enhance and make beautiful the appearance of the street buildings. The city shall be laid out so that it will have its business locality, tenement and residential districts, with its large uptown family hotels and its commercial downtown hotels. The business area shall be strictly confined to certain localities, and it shall not be permitted that business houses or stores of any kind will be located in residential districts as at the present day. The locality selected for residential purposes will be kept strictly for that purpose. Districts shall be set aside for all kinds of resident purposes. There shall be the Workingman's [sic] District, laid out in avenues, with their tenement blocks and residences, and every alternate square shall be a small park or breathing space. Then there shall be what will be termed the Boulevarded District, where the streets shall all be laid out of great width, with boulevards extending up the centre and sides of these streets, planted with shrubbery and flowers, and every alternate block will be a garden square, left for the recreation and health of the citizens. Great tenement blocks and residences of handsome design shall face upon these boulevards. Then there will be what may be termed the Palatial District, that will be laid out with grand avenues and boulevards throughout its length, and ornamented with groups of statuary, fountains, shrubbery and flowers, and everything that wealth can provide to beautify, and in this district the restrictions in building will be of such a nature that all residences will have to be of a design that will partake of a palace of grandeur, where only those who are blessed with great wealth can afford to live and keep up such habitation.

In the business districts the present buildings that line the street will all have vanished before the march of progress and in their places new structures will be re-erected. The business streets will be extended and widened. There will be sub-roadways constructed under the level of the present roadways, and the street car traffic will all be removed to these sub-streets, so that it will give more feeling of breadth and freedom, thereby enhancing to the mind the grandeur of the architecture of the mercantile buildings, and all along the line of these business streets will be erected blocks of commercial grandeur. It shall be required that all mercantile, office and other business buildings will be built absolutely fire-proof and in their construction shall be required the use of material that will be invented by that time, which will be almost impervious to heat or weather decay. Each business block will be restricted in building to a certain height, and every building will have its exposed facades, that are seen from the public thoroughfare, built of materials of such tone of colour as the Commissioners may determine. This will be insisted upon to brighten up the street and lend charm to the enriched details of architectural designs. Every building in itself will be a masterpiece of architecture, and possibly of some new style that may be developed by that time, or they may be designed in conformity with well-known styles of architecture of the past, with enriched colonnaded stories, or designed of other forms that will lend breadth and dignity, relieved with handsome carved embellishment. Some designs will partake of a classic form with its grandly proportioned facades of pedestal, column and enriched entablatures, while other designs will rely upon their quiet treatment in repose of well proportioned displays of enriched belt courses, spandriels [sic] and cornices, relieved with statue and bold relief carvings.

It will be further enacted, so as not to interfere with the splendour of the street architecture, that once the buildings are completed and finally accepted by the Board of Expert Commissioners, no alterations or additions will be permitted that will mar the designs of their facades. Then as the business district is built up, further accommodation for the growing business community will have to be provided and every available space will be made use of, and so great will be the demand that plans will be devised for using some of the spaces at the intersection of the business streets. The City Corporation will see the necessity to grant privileges under corporation restrictions, to build over and occupy these spaces, to assist in providing further accommodation. Great buildings will be erected, supported on archways springing over the roadway and sidewalks, so as not to interfere with the traffic, the adjacent corner blocks will be conformed to fit in and form in design a harmonious whole. These buildings, from their appearance and location, shall be called Great Tower Buildings, and they shall be built up to a height of many stories above the surrounding buildings, and of splendid design. The upper portions shall be monumental in appearance, and the lower portions immediately over the roadways will be designed to partake in appearance of triumphal arches. These Tower buildings shall be erected for business purposes, which will make them of great demand on account of their location and their breadth of sides facing four ways, opposite the streets running at right angles from their location, which will ensure to their occupants plenty of light and air. These buildings shall be erected from time to time, not only for commercial purposes, but as monuments to commemorate passing events in the history of the city, whose commanding appearance and beauty of design shall be the admiration of all who see them. Communication will be had from the street level to the upper portions by continuous travelling elevators, which will be installed in the angles of these buildings and will travel from the street level to the many floors above.

Then to make convenient communication from one to other of these Tower Buildings so that it will not necessitate people having to descend to the street level, there will be erected elevated steel enclosed bridgeways, which shall be constructed above the level of the other buildings in such a manner as will not hinder any light or sunshine to the highways and for this reason will run in a diagonal manner over the surrounding buildings, and made connecting from the angle of one tower building to the other. These bridges will be fitted up with compressed air noiseless tramway cars, that all possible noise may be avoided and so that all those who do business in these buildings can be transported from one to the other with the greatest possible despatch.

It must be admitted, with the innovation of these great tower buildings, that a marked change will be introduced in street architecture, and so impressive and lasting will be the appearance of these monumental buildings, standing majestically as they will, overlooking the roadways and the city generally, and probably lasting on and into other generations, that the inhabitants of the following age, in looking back for a name to designate its architecture of that time, will, in my opinion, be so impressed with these great tower buildings as to name the age that they were erected in "The Great Tower Age."

With all these growing changes, the harbor and the island will likewise be improved, in keeping with the dignity of the large and important city. It will of necessity be required that the railway tracks that pass along the city front shall be elevated to the higher level, so that the railways may enter the city on a level to suit the convenience of the passenger traffic. These track elevations will extend from beyond the Humber river in the west to beyond the Don river in the

east, and at each of these terminals will be freight yards for the reception of ordinary merchandise to suit convenience in delivery for the west or east sides of the city. Under these elevated railroad beds, between the intersecting of the cross streets, will be built cold storage and other warehouses, where special goods will be delivered from the cars above, lowered by elevators down into these warehouses beneath. Large railway stations of handsome architectural design will be erected. The Esplanade bordering the bay immediately in front of the city will be widened out and all along the water-front new docks will be built of permanent material. A new road will be built to accommodate the tremendous traffic that will be carried on.

Then, to further beautify the Esplanade, a Park Drive will also be constructed along the line of the water-front. This driveway will connect with the other park and boulevard driveways of the city and be extended to the Island by drawbridges over the Eastern and Western Gaps, where it shall be further connected with a system of Island Park driveways, the whole being artistically laid out and ornamented in the best of landscape garden style that will lend attraction throughout its entire length and so one might continue this article and allow his imagination to still run on, but as all things must end I might say.

In conclusion may I venture to wish that some at least of the improvements that have been suggested by my imagination may yet take form, and that they may be started, and possibly some of us may yet live to see them finished, if not in whole, at least in part.

APPENDIX B

INVENTORY OF BOOKS OWNED BY E.J. LENNOX

Archives of Ontario
Lennox Collection

Allen, Fred H. *The Great Cathedrals of the World.* Boston, 1886.

Art for All and Decorations. V.I., no date.

Bethlehem Steel Company. *Bethlehem Sections.* Bethlehem, Pa. (c. 1913) (Catalog s-40).

Brandon, Raphael. *An Analysis of Gothic Architecture.* London, 1860.

Colling, J.K. *Art Foliage.* Boston, 1880.

Cook, Carson C. *Rate Inlaid Interest Tables and Account Averager.* Plain edition, Toronto, 1888.

Davie, W. Galsworthy. *Old English Doorways.* London, 1903.

Folio of portraits of Spanish and Portuguese architecture, text in German.

Garner, Thomas. *Domestic Architecture of England during the Tudor Period.* London. 3 vols. 1908–1909.

Gotch, J. Alfred. *Architecture of the Renaissance in England.* London, 1894.

Indiana Limestone Company. *ILCO Details Bedford.* No date.

Jones, H.H. *System of Drainage Tables.* Toronto, 1888.

Kidder, Frank E. *Architect's and Builder's Pocketbook.* 14th ed. New York, 1904.

Latham, Charles. *In English Homes.* 2nd ed. London, 1907,

Lessing, Otto. *Ausgefuhrte Bauornamente der Neuzeit.* Berlin, 1884.

Licht, Hugo. *Architektur Deutschlands.* Berlin, 1882.

Mott, J.L. Iron Works. *Imperial Porcelain Lavatories.* New York, 1900.

———. *Flush-Valves for Water Closets, Urinals and Slop Sinks.* New York, 1901.

Nicolai, Herrmann Gearg. *Das Ornament der Italienischer Kunst des XV Jahrhunderts.* Weil, no date.

Otto, Karlvon. *The Elements of Graphic Statics.* London, 1895.

Paley, F.A. *A Manual of Gothic Moldings.* 4th ed. London, 1878.

Parker, Harry. *Simplified Engineering for Architects and Builders.* New York, 1938.

Raschdroff, Otto. *Palast-Architektur Von Oberitalien und Poscana.* Berlin, no date.

Ricker, N. Clifford. *Elementary graphic statics and the construction of trussed roofs.* New York, 1892.

Robinson, Joseph Barlow. *Architectural Foliage.* New York, no date.

Rosengarten, A. *A handbook of architectural styles.* London, 1880.

Schweinfurth, Julius A. *Sketches Abroad.* Boston, 1888.

Selfridge, Russell. *Modern French Architecture.* Boston, 1899.

Sharpe, Edmund. *The Seven Periods of English Architecture.* 2nd ed. London, 1871,

Starrett, L.S. Company. *Fine Mechanical Tools.* Athol, Mass., 1924 (Catalog no. 23).

Stillson, Henry Leonard. *History of the ancient and honorable fraternity of free and accepted masons and concordant orders.* Boston, 1891.

Thauwald, C.F. and Co. *Sketches of Wood-Mantels and Fire Places.* Cincinnati, no date.

Thorpe, John. *The Glass Dealer's Ready Reckoner.* St. Helen's, Lancashire, 1884.

Tiffany, H.S. *Digest of Depreciations.* Chicago, 1890.

Uhde, Constantin. *Baudemkmaeler in Spanien und Portugal.* Berlin, 1891.

———. *Baudemkmaeler in Spanien und Portugal.* Berlin, no date.

Ware, William Rotch. *Door and Window Grilles in Bronze and Iron.* Boston, 1902.

Weale, John. *Quarterly Papers on Architecture.* London, 1844. Vols. 1 and 2.

———. *Divers Works of Early Masters in Christian Decoration.* 2 vols. London, 1846.

Withers, Frederick Clarke. *Church Architecture.* New York, 1873.

City of Toronto Archives
Lennox Collection

de Graff, S. *The Modern Geometrical Stair-Builder's Guide, Being a Plain Practical system of Hand-Railing, Embracing all its Necessary Details, and Geometrically Illustrated by Twenty-two Steel Engravings.* Philadelphia, 1856.

Meyer, F.S. *A Handbook of Ornament.* London, no date.

Newlands, J. *The Carpenter and Joiner's Assistant.* 1865.

GLOSSARY

Aisle   Part of a church generally running parallel to the nave, separated from the nave by an arcade.

Ambulatory   An aisle surrounding the outside of a choir or chancel.

Apse   The semicircular termination of a church or long building.

Arcade   A series of arches carried on columns or piers, attached to or independent of a wall.

Ashlar   Squared building stone.

Balustrade   Railing, supported by a row of balusters (short posts), used on a terrace or gallery.

Barrel vault   A continuous unbroken arched ceiling or roof of stone or brick.

Batter   The vertical slope of a wall toward the body of a building.

Battlement   A parapet with notches at regular intervals.

Bay   Any number of similar major vertical divisions of a large building.

Belvedere   A small lookout tower on the roof of a building.

Boss   An ornamental knob-like projection at the intersection of ribs in a vault or ceiling.

Bracket   A support that carries a projecting weight.

Buttress   Masonry or brickwork built to support a structure by opposing outward thrust.

Capital   The uppermost element of a column or pilaster.

Cartouche   A rounded convex surface surrounded by highly ornamental scrollwork.

Caryatid   A female figure used as a column or pilaster to carry an entablature.

Casement   A window that opens on hinges.

Chancel   Part of the church reserved for clergy and choir, usually at the east end.

Choir   The eastern part of the church that accommodates the singers.

Clerestory   Row of windows above side aisles, providing direct light to the nave of a church.

Clustered pier   Sometimes called compound pier: a pier composed of a number of shafts.

Coffer   Ceiling decoration comprising sunken square or polygonal ornamental panels.

Colonnade   A series of columns carrying arches or an entablature.

Corbel   A projection jutting out from wall to support a beam or other structure.

Corbelling   A series of stepped corbels to support architectural elements such as turrets, chimneys, projecting windows etc.

Corinthian order   One of the orders of classical architecture characterized by acanthus leaves and a square abacus.

Cornice The upper member of an entablature or any ornamental moulding that projects along the top of a wall, pillar, or building.

Dado The finish of the lower part of an interior wall to approximately waist level.

Diaper work Surface decoration of repeating pattern of square and/or lozenge shapes.

Doric order The simplest of the classical orders, having a plain capital - column - and no base.

Dormer window A vertical window in a sloping roof covered by own roof.

Elevation The external face of a building; also architectural drawing showing vertical plane of a structure.

Engaged columns Columns attached to, or partly built into, a wall.

Entablature In classical architecture, the upper part of an order above the capital comprising architrave, frieze, and cornice.

Façade The front of a building.

Finial An ornament at the apex of gable, pediment, or pinnacle.

Fluting Shallow vertical concave grooves on the shaft of a column or pilaster.

Fretwork Geometrically composed perforated ornamental work.

Frieze That part of the entablature between the architrave and cornice. Also refers to long horizontal ornamented elements at a high level.

Gable Triangular wall at the end of a sloped roof.

Gallery In church architecture, an upper storey opening on to the nave or sanctuary.

Groin Ridges formed by the intersection of two vaults.

Half-timber A form of timber construction in which exposed timber skeleton is filled in by brick, clay, or other material. A type of roof construction that relies on brackets and struts to support the rafters.

Hammer-beam roof A type of roof construction that relies on horizontal projecting brackets and braces to support struts and exposed rafters.

Hipped roof A roof with sides and ends sloped.

Ionic order One of the orders of classical architecture characterized by volutes.

Keep The main tower of a castle.

Keystone Central stone of a masonry arch.

Light A window, particularly a small one.

Lintel Horizontal member over an opening that carries weight of structure above.

Loggia A roofed gallery or arcade open on at least one side.

Monitor A raised part of the roof that provides light and ventilation.

Mullion A vertical bar dividing a window into separate lights.

Nave The central area of a church, separated from side aisles by arcades or colonnades.

Obelisk A tall tapering shaft, usually of granite, square or rectangular in section, terminating in a pyramid; original to ancient Egypt.

Oculus A round window.

Order Refers to the five categories of classical architecture: Doric, Tuscan, Ionic, Corinthian, or Composite, distinguished by the style of base, capital, and entablature.

Oriel A bay window, especially found on upper storeys.

Panel An area of material enclosed by a frame or border.

Parapet A low protective wall along the edge of a roof.

Pediment A low-pitched gable above a portico or above doors, windows, etc., which may be straight-sided or curved segmentally.

Peep An aperture for looking through.

Pier Square masonry support from which arches spring in an arcade.

Pilaster A shallow pier or rectangular column projecting slightly from a wall.

Pinnacle A small cone-shaped structure crowning a spire.

Plinth A projecting base of a building or column pedestal.

Porte-cochère A decorative shelter at the main entrance of a building extending over a driveway.

Portico Attached roofed space at the entrance or centrepiece of the façade of a building, supported by columns, often having a pediment.

Quoins Dressed rectangular stones laid alternately long and short at the corners of an elevation to highlight the corners of a building.

Rib A projecting arch-like member of a vault; used decoratively or to strengthen the structure.

Rock-faced Stone hewn to appear like rough blocks straight from the quarry.

Rose window Circular window with patterned tracery radiating symmetrically from the centre.

Rustication Various forms of ashlar laid with deep joints: called banded if the channelling is only horizontal.

Sanctuary Area around the main altar of a church.

Scagliola Material such as cement, plaster, or marble dust used to simulate marble.

Strapwork Decoration comprising interlaced geometric bands, similar to fretwork.

String course A horizontal band, flush with or projecting beyond the surface of a building.

Terracotta Fired clay used for decorative panels and facing. Often glazed in various colours for ornaments and veneers.

Tracery Ornamental intersecting work in the upper part of windows or in panels or screens.

Transept The transverse arms that usually cross the body of the church between the nave and the choir.

Turret Small slender tower, often beginning some distance above the ground level.

Vault An arched structure made of brick or stone.

NOTES

ABBREVIATIONS

AO   Archives of Ontario
CTA   City of Toronto Archives
NA   National Archives
OHA   Ontario Hydro Archives

Preface

1 See E. Arthur, *Toronto, No Mean City*, 3rd ed., for further information.

Introduction

1 See C.B. Robinson, *History of Toronto and County of York*, vol. 1 (1885), 354.
2 The Mechanics' Institute, built in 1854 by Cumberland and Storm, held lectures and classes to further the education of members of the various trades. In 1884, the building and its holdings were given to the Free Library Board by the Institute to become Toronto's first public library.
3 C.B. Robinson, *History of Toronto and County of York*, vol. 1 (1885), 354.
4 Ibid.
5 E. Arthur, *Toronto, No Mean City*, 248.
6 T.A. Reed, "Toronto's Early Architects," *JRAIC*, February 1950, 50.
7 C.B. Robinson, *History of Toronto and County of York*, vol. 1 (1885), 354.
8 Colin Vaughan, now a well-known television political commentator, was a practising architect. He is still actively interested in architectural preservation.
9 C. Vaughan, "Homage to a Home," *Globe and Mail*, Fanfare, 1 June 1977, 7.
10 R. Hyman, "Edward James Lennox, The Architect Who Fought for His City Hall," *Globe and Mail*, 6 January 1966, 21.
11 At the time of Lennox's death, in addition to his home, he owned the following real estate: 32 Russell Hill Road; 612–16 Bloor Street West; 1232–36 Bloor Street West; and 546 Yonge Street.
12 Lennox maintained his Orange convictions to the very end. His will, dated July 1932, stipulated that should any of his beneficiaries marry anyone of the Roman Catholic faith, he or she would be cut off from his estate.
13 In 1922, the practice was reopened as "E.J. Lennox & Son Architects." Lennox, however, was a member of the firm in name only. After E.J. died, in 1933, Edgar, who was a somewhat reluctant architect, shut the firm down. The few drawings that remain from 1922 to 1933 belong to the hand of Edgar.
14 Obituary, *Toronto Telegram*, 17 April 1933, 2. A number of technical books that belonged to Lennox are now held in the Archives of Ontario and in the City of Toronto Archives (see Appendix B).

Chapter 1: Early Practice

1 *Globe*, "Tenders Wanted" column, May 15, 1876, 3.
2 S.G. Curry, in an article title "Architecutre: Looking Back," *Construction*, June 1927, 175, lists Grant & Dirk; James & Connelly; Langley, Langley & Burke; Almond E. Paul; Smith & Gemmell; W.G. Storm; Kivas Tully; William Kauffman; William Irving; Lalor & Martin; McDougall & darling; David Roberts; William Stewart; Walter P. Strickland; R.C. Windeyer. See E. Arthur, *Toronto: No Mean City*, for more information.
3 Based on the nineteenth-century "calls for tender" data bank developed by Toronto architect Kent Rawson.
4 C.P. Mulvany, *Toronto, Past and Present until 1882*, 132–33.
5 Minutes of the Standing Committee on Walks and Gardens, 16 March 1876, City of Toronto.
6 Report of the Standing Committee on Walks and Gardens, 19 June 1876, City of Toronto.
7 McCaw & Lennox's letter was dated 4 December 1876; from the Minutes of the Standing Committee on Walks and Gardens, 11 December 1876, City of Toronto.
8 *Globe*, "Tenders Wanted" column, 6 April 1878, 7.
9 Ibid., 17 August 1878, 5.
10 C.B. Robinson, *History of Toronto and County of York*, vol. 1 (1885), 315.
11 *Daily Globe*, "Tenders Wanted" column, 20 December 1879, 7,
12 C.P. Mulvany, *Toronto Past and Present until 1882*, 113.
13 *Globe*, "Tenders Wanted" column, 30 March 1880, 3; and 31 March 1881, 7.
14 Ibid., 24 July 1880, 9; and 24 January 1881, 7.
15 Ibid., 29 April 1881, 3.
16 *Toronto Telegram*, "Tenders Wanted" column, 6 November 1880, 2.
17 *Globe*, "Tenders Wanted" column, 11 November 1880, 7.
18 Ibid., 12 November 1881, 10.

19 Ibid., 18 February 1882, 11.

20 Patricia McHugh in *Toronto Architecture*, 37, indicated that the Standard Woollen Company, 237 Front Street, may have been designed by Lennox.

21 *Globe*, "Tenders Wanted" column, 19 October 1882, 5.

22 C.B. Robinson, *History of Toronto and County of York*, vol. 1 (1885), 316.

23 Ibid.

24 Building Permit #194, 9 December 1882, for the building of semi-detached houses for Mrs. Bilton on Gerrard Street.

25 From 1894 to its demolition in 1948, the house was occupied by the Reverend Cody, who married Mr. Henry E. Clarke's daughter, the very same Canon Cody for whom Lennox would later build St.Paul's Anglican Church on Bloor Street East.

26 Building Permit #195, December 9, 1882, for the building of a residence on the east side of Jarvis for H.E. Clarke. Plans and elevations in the Archives of Ontario are dated 1882.

27 "The Building Trade," *Globe*, 3 March 1883, 4

28 C.B. Robinson, *History of Toronto and County of York*, vol. 1, 376.

29 Chester Daniel was the father of two Canadians who brought honour to their country. Vincent Massey, a statesman and great promoter of the arts, holds the distinction of being the first Canadian-born governor general. Vincent would add another first to his long list of achievements. After Canada's right to pursue an independent foreign policy was ratified at the Imperial Conference of 1923, Canada established its first embassy in Washington in 1927 (J.A. Lower, *Canada*, 169–70). Vincent Massey was appointed as Canada's first permanent ambassador to the United States. Vincent's brother Raymond was even more famous, though he took a different avenue. Raymond left Canada for the United States to seek fame and fortune on the boards of Broadway and later on in the film industry. He was highly successful and ironically gained great fame by playing the role of Abraham Lincoln on film.

30 *Globe*, "Tenders Wanted" column, 28 April 1883, 11.

31 P. McHugh, *Toronto Architecture*, 79.

32 Specifications, 2 August 1884, AO, Lennox Collection, Box MU 1416.

33 V.L. Russell, *Mayors of Toronto*, vol. 1, 93.

34 C.B. Robinson, *History of Toronto and County of York*, vol. 1 (1885), 355.

35 E. Arthur, *Toronto, No Mean City*, 178.

36 Appears in the 1886 City Directory as a completed building.

Chapter 2: Toronto's Third City Hall

1 Letter to chairman of Court House Committee dated 13 June 1887. CTA, Legal Dept. Records, RG 19, Box 2, 9.

2 Ibid.

3 Lennox also reported the buildings in plan were "not as conveniently laid out as one might have expected . . . chambers or private rooms have been placed in awkward and inconvenient places … court rooms were not sufficiently lighted …" and so on. Letter to chairman of Court House Committee dated 13 June 1887.

4 R. Hall, *A Century To Celebrate*, 30.

5 J. Fleming et al, *A Dictionary of Architecture*, 237.

6 See Appendix B for list of books belonging to Edward James Lennox. The books made their way to the Archives of Ontario by way of the late Alice Alison, one of the key members of the "Save the Old City Hall" group of concerned citizens when the building was threatened with demolition, and Mary Eckardt Gooderham, grand-daughter to E.J. Lennox.

7 *Toronto Municipal and County Buildings*, brochure issued by members of Court House Committee, 1889.

8 *Toronto Mail*, 6 April 1888, 1.

9 *Telegram*, "Tenders Wanted" column, 14 July 1888, 8.

10 *Toronto Municipal and County Buildings*, brochure.

11 Ibid.

12 Application for registration to practice as an architect, dated 24 September 1931.

13 "Laying the Stone," *Toronto Mail*, 23 November 1891, 1.

14 Letter from Lennox to the chairman of the Building Committee, 12 May 1892, CTA, Legal Dept. Records, RG 19, Box 2., 151.

15 Letter to Sylvester Neelon, July 2, 1892, CTA, Legal Dept. Records, RG 19, Box 2, 151.

16 "Captain Neelon Bounced by Midnight Band," *Evening Telegram*, 9 September 1892, 2.

17 *The Canadian Architect and Builder* was established in 1888 to promote architectural professionalism and is an important source of information for the study of architectural history. See K. Crossman, *Architecture in Transition: From Art to Practice, 1885–1906*, for further discussion.

18 *Canadian Architect and Builder*, April 1899, 69.

19 D. Cohen, "Master Builder," *Toronto Star Sunday Magazine*, 23 March1980, 22.

20 R. Hyman, "The architect who fought for his City Hall," *Globe and Mail*, 6 January 1966, 21.

21 *Toronto Municipal and County Buildings*, brochure.

22 Unpublished description of the Robert McCausland window by Robert McCausland Ltd., 11 January 1946, CTA files.

23 "Toronto City Hall," *Canadian Architect and Builder*, October 1899, 194–95.

24 E. Arthur, *Toronto, No Mean City*, 205.

Chapter 3: The City Hall Years

1 *Globe*, "Tenders Wanted" column, 19 June 1886, 14.

2 P. McHugh, *Toronto Architecture*, 34.

3 *Globe*, "Tenders Wanted" column, 17 September 1886, 6.

4 *Canadian Architect and Builder*, February 1888, 4.

5 W. Dendy, *Lost Toronto*, 133.

6 *Evening Telegram*, "Tenders Wanted" column, 15 September 1887, 1.

7 Specifications for the house are dated October 1886, AO, Lennox Collection, Box MU 1416.

8 W. Dendy and W. Kilbourn, *Toronto Observed*, 149.

9 P. McHugh, *Toronto Architecture*, 226.

10 *Canadian Architect and Builder*, February 1888, "Contracts Awarded" column, 6.

11 Ibid.

12 Ibid.

13 P. McHugh, *Toronto Architecture*, 168.

14 *Globe*, 18 July 1889, "Tenders Wanted" column, 3.

15 *Canadian Architect and Builder*, December 1889, 143.

16 T. Ritchie, *Canada Builds*, 323.

17 *Contract Record*, 12 April 1890, 11.

18 M. Hunschberger et al, *Romanesque Toronto*, 15.

19 Listed in 1891 City Directory as "under construction."

20 Building Permit #796, 25 April 1892 – for the Beard Estate.

21 A. Sobolak, "A Lennox Folly: The Beard Building," *ACT – Newsletter*, November 1988, 14.

22 "To Demolish Lennox Folly," *Evening Telegram*, 21 May 1935, 12.

23 J. Fleming et al, *The Penguin Dictionary of Architecture*, 266.

24 Letter from E.J. Lennox to H.A. Massey dated 30 December 1892, NA, Massey Family Papers, MG 32 A1 Reel C-9204.

25 Letter from E.J. Lennox to H.A. Massey dated November 16, 1892, National Archives, Massey Family Papers, MG 32 A1 Reel C-9204.

26 P. McHugh, *Toronto Architecture*, 90.

27 *Canadian Architect and Builder*, February 1897, 37.

28 R. Hall, *A Century to Celebrate*, 35.

29 J.M.S. Careless, *Toronto to 1918*, 149.

Chapter 4: Palaces and Pantheons

1 Perspective of proposed building, *Canadian Architect and Builder*, August 1900, illus. 8.

2 In particular, American architect Louis H. Sullivan (1856–1924).

3 S.M. Green, *American Art*, 319.

4 R. Card, *The Ontario Association of Architects, 1870–1950*, 20.

5 K. Crossman, *Architecture in Transition*, 94.

6 See Arthur, *Toronto, No Mean City*, for more information.

7 The King Edward Hotel was first called the Toronto Hotel. It was named the King Edward after Edward VII's accession to the throne in 1901.

8 A.S. Thompson, *Jarvis Street*, 170.

9 Those listed as directors were William Henry Beatty, Hugh N. Baird, Duncan Coulson, L.J. Forget, George Gooderham, Edward Gurney, John Hoskin, André S. Irving, Robert Jaffray, Albert E. Kemp, John Woodburn Langmuir, John Herbert Mason, Wilmot D. Matthews, Edmund B. Osler, Byron E. Walker, David Wilkie, and Frederick Wyld. Cited as an item in the *Mail and Empire*, 16 May 1899, in W.A. Craick's unpublished manuscript, "Toronto Papers," vol 20, 14, Baldwin Room holdings at the Metropolitan Toronto Reference Library.

10 Mr. George McConkey, entrepreneur and restaurateur, was a steady client of Lennox's. In 1889 Lennox was responsible for renovating 29 King Street West, "lately occupied as a jewellery store by C. & J. Allen," to be used as a complete confectionery store, lunch rooms, and restaurant (*Globe*, "Tenders Wanted" column, 23 January 1889, 7). According to Arthur, *Toronto, No Mean City*, 179, "the Ontario Association of Architects moved their dinner meetings from Webb's restaurant to McConkey's, the latter being described as more elegant." By 1899 McConkey's had become so popular that McConkey decided to expand his operations to include 31–33 King Street West. He again called on Lennox and the result was the much-admired Palm Garden.

11 C.D. Lennox, ed., *Toronto Architectural Eighteen Club, First Annual Exhibition, 1901*, Exhibits #168 and #173.

12 On 5 February 1906 more than 700 men crowded into the restaurant to listen to Dr. Booker T. Washington (1856–1915), one of the most celebrated U.S. reformers, educators, authors, and lecturers, address the Canadian Club. Washington's extensive writings include an autobiography, *Up from Slavery* (1901).

13 Building Permit #143, 17 December 1901.

14 "The Toronto Hotel," *Globe*, 7 July 1900, 10.

15 Building Permit #346, 2 April 1902.

16 See Illus. 70.

17 W. Dendy and W. Kilbourn, *Toronto Observed*, 159.

18 A.S. Thompson, *Jarvis Street*, 171.

19 E. Arthur, *Toronto, No Mean City*, 200.

20 Drawings dated July 1901, AO, Lennox Collection.

21 Existence of a building permit, dated 23 October 1902, recorded in Toronto Historical Board, Buildings Inventory Files.

22 Building permit #316, 21 September 1902.

23 P. McHugh, *Toronto Architecture*, 234.

24 Drawings dated June 1903, AO, Lennox Collection.

25 Listed in the 1903 City Directory.

26 L.B. Martyn, *Aristocratic Toronto*, 140.
27 E. Arthur, *Toronto, No Mean City*, 3rd ed., 135.
28 Building Permit #1199, 27 May 1903.
29 Careless, *Toronto to 1918*, 152.
30 Listed in Lennox's day book, as drawings dated 10 June 1903, AO, Lennox Collection, Box MU 1432.
31 R.M. Stamp, *Bright Lights, Big City*, 21.
32 Letter from E.J. Lennox to Frederic Nicholls, Esq., vice-president and general manager Electrical Development Co. of Ontario, Ltd. (undated), OHA, Early Records Collection.
33 Letter from J.W. Langmuir, chairman of the Niagara Falls Park Commission, to Frederic Nicholls, indicating approval of Lennox's design, dated 4 January 1904, OHA, Early Records Collection.
34 Second Annual Report, Toronto, 27 January 1905, OHA, Early Records Collection,
35 The obelisk design was used again in Casa Loma and Postal Station "G."
36 Plans dated August 1904, AO, Lennox Collection.
37 *Electrical News*, June 1906, 136.
38 Electrical Development Co. Minute Book, 1906, 152, OHA, Early Records Collection.
39 Drawing dated August 1905. AO, Lennox Collection.
40 *Canadian Architect and Builder*, July 1906, 101.
41 Architectural "conditions" report prepared by Jill Taylor of Taylor-Hazell Architects, 39.
42 D. Richardson, *Beaux-Arts Toronto*, 3.
43 W. Dendy and W. Kilbourn, *Toronto Observed*, 179.
44 Drawing showing iron fence, dated June 1903, AO, Lennox Collection.
45 Drawing dated June 1905, AO, Lennox Collection.
46 Hampton Court and Hengrave Hall appear in illustrations in G. Garner, *Domestic Architecture in England during the Tudor Period* (1908), vol 2, part 2, plate CVL. This folio publication belonged to Lennox and is now in the Archives of Ontario, Lennox Collection, #39, Box MU 1431.
47 Building Permit #18643, 16 December 1909.
48 W. Dendy and W. Kilbourn, *Toronto Observed*, 179.
49 C. Stewart, *Gothic Architecture*, 213.
50 T. Copplestone, *Architecture, The Great Art of Building*, 44.
51 W. Dendy and W. Kilbourn, *Toronto Observed*, 182.
52 Based on information provided by Rand Sparling, son of architect William Frederick Sparling (1884–1940), who owned Casa Loma from 1925 to 1929.
53 Kiwanis Club of West Toronto, *Major General Sir Henry Mill Pellatt*, 5.
54 M. Litvak, "English Country House in Downtown Toronto," *The Antique Collector*, December 1985, 45.

Chapter 5: Last Works

1 *Contract Record*, 29 September 1909, 23.
2 Lennox specifications for reconstruction of the Ontario Parliament Buildings, 13, CTA, Lennox Collection, SC 48, Box 3.
3 *Contract Record*, 24 March 1909, 20.
4 Though a recent amalgamation of Western Hospital with Toronto General rendered Western's archival material inaccessible, information was provided by Mrs. Fee, a long-time member of the original Archives of Western Hospital.
5 "Lennox gave plans for St. Paul's Church," *Mail and Empire*, 19 April 1933, 4.
6 N. Nunn, *St. Paul's Church*, 5.
7 Commemorative plaque on St. Paul's, just west of the main door.
8 N. Nunn, *St. Paul's Church*, 3.
9 "Design and Construction of the New St. Paul's church, Toronto," *Contract Record*, 4 June 1913 (reprint).
10 Ibid.
11 Listed in the 1913 City Directory.
12 D. Johnson, "City Holds Up Riverdale Post Office Takeover," *Seven News*, 29 November 1975, 3.
13 Lennox reported his intention to build in the *Contract Record*, 16 July 1913, 78. "Residence, cost $18,000. Walmer and Davenport, for E.J. Lennox, 164 Bay Street, architect and general contractor, owner. Masonry and stone, Page & Co., Queen's Park. 2 1/2 storeys, 60 x 100, stone, structural steel and brick construction."
14 L.B Martyn, *Aristocratic Toronto*, 214.
15 Drawing in Achives of Ontario, Lennox Collection, dated June 1914
16 *Construction*, August 1915, 337.
17 "The Excelsior Life Building," *Construction*, March 1916, 71.
18 "Mainly Constructional" column, *Contract Record*, May 1915, 522.
19 "The Excelsior Life Building," *Construction*, March 1916, 71.

BIBLIOGRAPHY

BOOKS AND MONOGRAPHS

General Works

Copplestone, T. *Architecture, The Great Art of Building*. Middlesex, 1969.

Fleming, J., Honour H., and N. Pevsner. *A Dictionary of Architecture*. Harmondsworth, 1976.

Hitchcock, H.-R. *Architecture: Nineteenth and Twentieth Centuries*. Harmondsworth, 1967.

Hughes, J.Q., and N. Lynton. *Renaissance Architecture*. Simpson's History of Architectural Development, vol. 4. London, 1962.

Pevsner, N. *Pioneers of Modern Design*. Harmondsworth, 1960.

Stewart, C. *Early Christian, Byzantine and Romanesque Architecture*. Simpson's History of Architectural Development, vol 2. London, 1964.

———. *Gothic Architecture*. Simpson's History of Architectural Development. Vol. 3. London, 1964.

Canada

Crossman, K. *Architecture in Transition: From Art to Practice, 1885–1906*. Kingston and Montreal, 1987.

Gowans, A. *Building Canada, An Architectural History of Canadian Life*. Toronto, 1966.

Johnston, P.J. Chenier, P.R.L. *Index of Canadian Architect and Builder, 1888–1908*. Ottawa, 1984.

Lerner, L., and M. Williamson. *Art and Architecture in Canada: A Bibliography and Guide to the Literature*. Toronto, 1991.

Lower, J.A. *Canada, An Outline History*. Toronto, 1973.

Maitland, L. *The Queen Anne Revival Style in Canadian Architecture*. Ottawa, 1990.

Mayran, P., and J. Bland. *Three Centuries of Architecture in Canada*. Montreal, 1971.

Ritchie, T. *Canada Builds*. Toronto,1967.

Wallace, W.S. *The Macmillan Dictionary of Canadian Biography*. Toronto, 1963.

Ontario

Card, R. *The Ontario Association of Architects 1890–1950*. Toronto, 1950.

Fram, M. *Ontario Ministry of Culture and Recreation Report on the Historical Background and Current Status of the Toronto Power Generating Station at Niagara Falls*. Toronto, 1978.

Seibel, G.A. *Ontario's Niagara Parks: A History*. Niagara Falls, 1985.

Toronto

Adam, G. Mercer. *Toronto Old and New*. Toronto, 1891.

Armstrong, F.H. *City in the Making – Progress, People and Perils in Victorian Toronto*. Toronto and Oxford, 1988.

Arthur, E. *Toronto, No Mean City*. 2nd ed. Toronto, 1974; and 3rd ed. revised (S. Otto), Toronto, 1986.

Arthur, E. *From Front Street to Queen's Park*. Toronto, 1979.

Beszedits, S. *Eminent Toronto Architects of the Past, Their Lives and Works*. Toronto, 1983.

Board of Trade Souvenir Number. Toronto, 1893.

Careless, J.M.S. *Toronto to 1918, An Illustrated History*. Toronto, 1984

Clark, C.S. *Of Toronto the Good*. Montreal, 1898.

Dendy, W. *Lost Toronto*. Toronto, 1978.

Dendy, W., and W. Kilbourn. *Toronto Observed – Its Architecture, Patrons, and History*. Toronto, 1986.

Denison, J. *Casa Loma and the Man Who Built It*. Erin, 1982.

Denison, M. *Harvest Triumphant*. Toronto, 1949.

Dilse, P. *Toronto's Theatre Block: An Architectural History*. Toronto, 1989.

Gibson, S. *More Than an Island*. Toronto, 1984.

Glazebrook, G.P. de T. *The Story of Toronto*. Toronto, 1971.

Hall, R. *A Century to Celebrate, 1893–1993: The Ontario Legislative Building*. Toronto, 1993.

History of Toronto and County of York Ontario. Vol. 1. Toronto, 1885.

Hunchberger, M., et al. "Romanesque Toronto: A Photographic Exhibition of Late Nineteenth Century Architecture." Unpublished manuscript, University of Toronto, 1971.

Keefer A. *Terra Cotta – Artful Deceivers.* Toronto, 1990.

Lennox, C.D., ed. *Toronto Architectural Eighteen Club, First Annual Exhibition 1901.* Toronto, 1901.

———. *Toronto Architectural Eighteen Club, Second Annual Exhibition 1902.* Toronto, 1902.

Martyn, L.B. *Aristocratic Toronto.* Toronto, 1980.

McHugh, P. *Toronto Architecture, A City Guide.* Toronto, 1985.

Middleton, J.E. *The Municipality of the City of Toronto: A History.* Toronto and New York, 1923.

Mulvany, C.P. *Toronto Past and Present Until 1882.* Toronto, 1884.

Nunn, N.A. *St. Paul's Church One Hundred and Twenty-Fifth Anniversary 1842–1967.* Toronto, 1967.

Oreskovich, C. *The King of Casa Loma.* Toronto, 1982.

Richardson, D. *Beaux-Arts Toronto – Permanence and Change in Early 20th Century Architecture.* Toronto, 1973.

Russell, V.L. *Mayors of Toronto.* Erin, 1982.

Scadding, H., and C. Dent. *Toronto Past and Present, Historical and Descriptive,: A Memorial Volume for the Semi-Centennial of 1884.* Toronto, 1884.

Sir Henry Mill Pellatt, A Gentleman of Toronto, 1859–1939. Toronto, no date.

Stamp, R.M. *Bright Lights Big City, The History of Electricity in Toronto.* Toronto, 1991.

Thompson, A.S. *Jarvis Street, A Story of Triumph and Tragedy.* Toronto, 1980.

United States

Bush-Brown, A. *Louis Sullivan.* New York, 1960.

DeLong, D.G., H. Searing, and R.A.M. Stern. *American Architecture: Innovation and Tradition.* New York, 1986.

Gifford, D. *The Literature of Architecture.* New York, 1966.

Gowans, A. *Images of American Living.* New York, 1964.

Green, S.M. *American Art, A Historical Survey.* New York, 1966.

Hitchcock, H.-R. *The Architecture of H.H. Richardson and His Times.* 2nd ed. Hamden Conn., 1961.

Van Rensselaer, M.G. *Henry Hobson Richardson and His Works.* Boston and New York, 1888.

Weisman, W. *The Rise of an American Architecture.* New York, 1970.

England

Clifton-Taylor, A. *The Cathedrals of England.* London, 1967.

Kidson, P., P. Murray, and P. Thompson. *A History of English Architecture.* Harmondsworth, 1965.

Stanton, P. *Pugin.* London, 1971.

Summerson, J. *Architecture in Britain 1530–1830.* Harmondsworth, 1970.

ARTICLES

Cohen, D. "Master Builder," *Toronto Star Sunday Magazine,* 23 March 1980, 20-28.

Curry, S.G. "Architecture: Looking Back," *Construction,* June 1927, 175-183.

"Design and Construction of the New St. Paul's Church, Toronto, 1913," *Contract Record and Engineering Review,* 4 June 1913 (reprint n.p.).

"The Excelsior Life Building," *Construction,* March 1916, 71.

Fetherling, D. "The Man Who Built Casa Loma," *Financial Post Magazine,* December 1978, 37.

Hyman, R. "Edward James Lennox, The Architect Who Fought for His City Hall," *Globe and Mail,* 6 January 1966, 21.

Johnson, D. "City Holds Up Riverdale Post Office Takeover," *Seven New,* 29 November 1975, 3.

"Laying the Stone," *Toronto Mail,* 23 November 1891, 1.

"Lennox gave plans for St. Paul's Church," *Mail and Empire,* 19 April 1933.

Kalman, H. "Recent Literature on the History of Canadian Architecture," *Journal of the Society of Architectural Historians* 31, no. 4 (December 1972): 315–23.

Lemley, V. "The King of The Castle," *Key to Toronto*, 1974, 28–29.

Lennox, E.J. "What will the Architectural Appearance of Toronto be in the Year 2004 A.D.?," *Toronto's Christmas Magazine*, 15 December 1904, n.p.

Litvak, M. "English Country House in Downtown Toronto," *Antique Collector*, London, England, December 1985, 42–47.

Miller, R.A. "E.J. Lennox, Toronto Landmarks Show the Touch of a Master," *Real Estate News*, 22 April 1983, 6–7.

Nobbs, P.E. "Architecture in Canada," *Journal of the Royal Institute of British Architects*, S.3, 31 (1924): 199–211, 238–50.

Reed, T.A. "Toronto's Early Architects," *Journal of the Royal Architectural Institute of Canada*, 1950, 46–51.

Sobolak, A. "A Lennox Folly: The Beard Building," *Architectural Conservancy Toronto – Newsletter*, November 1988, 13–18.

"To Demolish Lennox Folly," *Evening Telegram*, 21 May 1935, 12.

Vaughan, C. "Homage to a Home," *Globe and Mail, Fanfare*, 1 June 1977, 8.

ARCHITECTURAL TRADE PUBLICATIONS

Canadian Architect and Builder
Construction
Contract Record
Contract Record & Engineering Review
Electrical News

NEWSPAPERS AND MAGAZINES

The Empire
The Globe
The Globe and Mail
Mail and Empire
Saturday Night
Seven News
The Telegram
The Toronto Star
The Toronto Mail

COLLECTIONS OF PAPERS, PHOTOGRAPHS AND DRAWINGS

Archives of Ontario
    The Lennox Collection of architectural drawings and related textual materials
    Photographic Records Collection
Casa Loma Archives
City of Toronto Archives
    Special Collections,
    Building Permits,
    City Directories,
    Vertical Files
    Council Minutes
Environment Canada
    Canadian Inventory of Historic Building
Metropolitan Toronto Reference Library
    Baldwin Room
        Mechanics' Institute annual reports
        Picture Collection
        Craick's Guide to Periodicals and Newspapers
    Arts Department
        Special Collections
        ARCHINDONT (an index to historic buildings in Ontario)
    General Information Services
        Newspaper Unit
National Archives of Canada
    The Massey papers
Ontario Hydro Archives
    Early Records Collection
    Photographic Collection
Toronto Historical Board
        Inventory of Buildings of Architectural and Historical Importance

INDEX

Note: Illustration page numbers are in italics.